Nature Guide to Rocky Mountain National Park

Rocky Mountain National Park: the Basics

History and Facts

Established: January 26, 1915

Visitors: About 3,000,000 annually

Designations: International Biosphere Reserve, 1976; National Scenic Byway, Trail Ridge Road, 1996; Globally Important Bird Area, 2000

Time zone: Mountain

Physical Features

Acreage: 265,800 acres, including 252,805 acres designated wilderness; tundra acres: 89,009; square miles: 415

Elevation: Highest national park in the United States; lowest point: 7,640 feet at Big Thompson River; highest point: 14,259 feet at Longs Peak; 60+ peaks over 12,000 feet; more than one-third of the park above tree line

Water resources: Lakes: 147; major rivers: 4—Colorado, Big Thompson, Cache la Poudre, and Fall; 450 miles of streams

Average annual precipitation: Estes Park, 14.79 inches; Grand Lake, 20.36 inches

Temperature range (F): -39° to 96°; lowest average, 18° in January; highest average, 79° in July

Plant species: 1,000+ species of vascular plants: 900+ species of wildflowers, 9 cone-bearing trees and shrubs, 58 other trees and shrubs, 101 grasses, 66 sedges, 47 ferns, 14 fern allies

Animal species: About 280 birds; 60 mammals; 11 fish (1 federally threatened); 1 reptile; 6 amphibians, including one federally endangered toad; 139 butterflies; 2,000+ invertebrates

Wildlife population estimates: Elk: 3,000 summer, 600–800 winter; bighorn sheep: 350+; black bears: 24; moose: 30–50; mountain lions: 20–30; coyotes: common; mule deer 500+

Facilities

Entrance stations: 4—Beaver Meadows, west of Estes Park, US 36; Fall River, west of Estes Park, US 34; Grand Lake, north of Grand Lake, US 34; Wild Basin, north of Allenspark, CO 7

Visitor centers: 5—Beaver Meadows, at Park Headquarters, US 36, west of Estes Park; Fall River, US 34, west of Estes Park; Moraine Park, on Bear Lake Road; Alpine, at Fall River Pass; Kawuneeche, on US 34, east of Grand Lake

Roads: Paved roads, 92 miles; unpaved roads, 28 miles. scenic roads: Trail Ridge Road ("All-America Road" and National Scenic Byway), Old Fall River Road, Bear Lake Road

Trails: 355 miles of trails including about 30 miles of Continental Divide National Scenic Trail and 260 miles of designated horse and pack trails

Campgrounds: 6,586 sites, including 4 types of backcountry sites: including individual, 197 sites; group, 21 sites; accessible, 1 site; and crosscountry areas, 16 sites; total 267 sites; Aspenglen, 54 sites; Glacier Basin, 150 sites; Longs Peak, 26 sites; Moraine Park, 245 sites; Timber Creek, 98 sites

Picnic areas: Over twenty-five areas with approximately 200 tables, including Endovalley with 32 tables and Sprague Lake with 27 tables

Nature Guide to Rocky Mountain National Park

A Pocket Field Guide

Ann and Rob Simpson

Published in cooperation with Rocky Mountain Nature Association

FALCON GUIDES

GUILFORD, CONNECTICUT
HELENA, MONTANA

AN IMPRINT OF GLOBE PEQUOT PRESS

FALCONGUIDES®

FalconGuides is an imprint of Globe Pequot Press.

Library of Congress Cataloging-in-Publication Data is available on file.

ISBN 978-0-7627-7063-2

Printed in the United States of America
10 9 8 7 6 5 4 3 2 1

Contents

ROCKY MOUNTAIN NATIONAL PARK

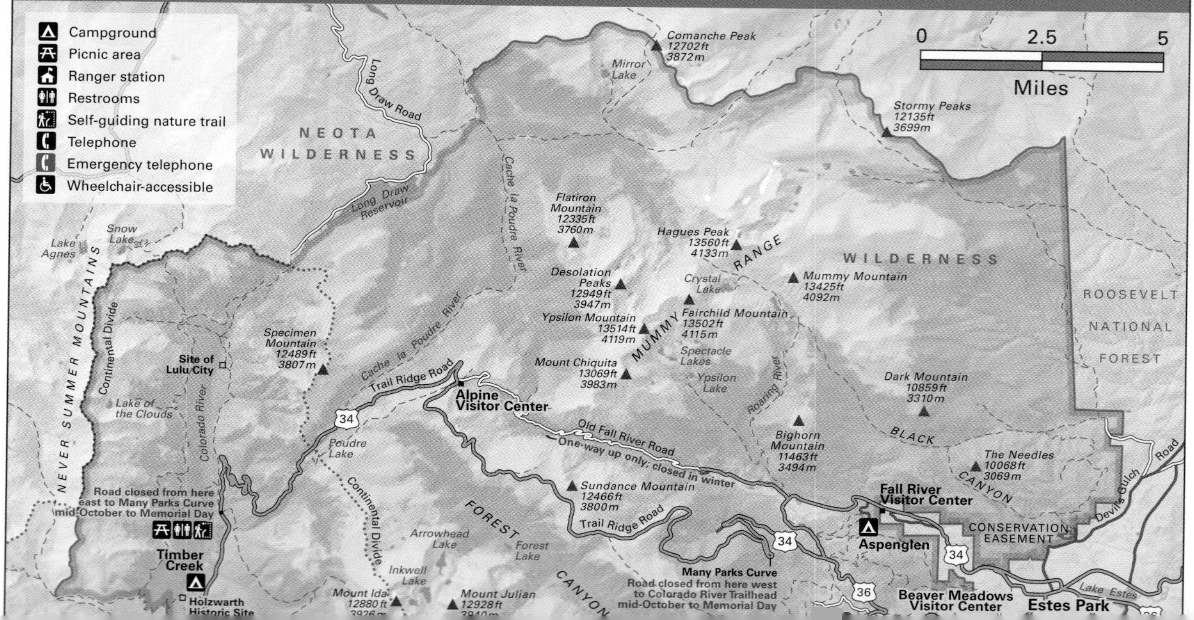

Campground
Picnic area
Ranger station
Restrooms
Self-guiding nature trail
Telephone
Emergency telephone
Wheelchair-accessible

0 2.5 5
Miles

NEOTA WILDERNESS
Long Draw Road
Long Draw Reservoir
Comanche Peak 12702ft 3872m
Mirror Lake
Stormy Peaks 12135ft 3699m
Cache la Poudre River
Flatiron Mountain 12335ft 3760m
Hagues Peak 13560ft 4133m
MUMMY RANGE
WILDERNESS
Desolation Peaks 12949ft 3947m
Crystal Lake
Mummy Mountain 13425ft 4092m
Fairchild Mountain 13502ft 4115m
Ypsilon Mountain 13514ft 4119m
Spectacle Lakes
Ypsilon Lake
Mount Chiquita 13069ft 3983m
Roaring River
ROOSEVELT NATIONAL FOREST
Dark Mountain 10859ft 3310m
BLACK CANYON
The Needles 10068ft 3069m
Devils Gulch Road
Lake Snow Lake
Lake Agnes
NEVER SUMMER MOUNTAINS
Continental Divide
Specimen Mountain 12489ft 3807m
Site of Lulu City
Cache la Poudre River
Trail Ridge Road
Alpine Visitor Center
Lake of the Clouds
Colorado River
34
Poudre Lake
Old Fall River Road
One-way up only; closed in winter
Bighorn Mountain 11463ft 3494m
Fall River Visitor Center
Sundance Mountain 12466ft 3800m
Road closed from here east to Many Parks Curve mid-October to Memorial Day
Continental Divide
FOREST CANYON
Trail Ridge Road
Aspenglen
CONSERVATION EASEMENT
Timber Creek
Arrowhead Lake
Forest Lake
Many Parks Curve
Road closed from here west to Colorado River Trailhead mid-October to Memorial Day
Inkwell Lake
Holzwarth Historic Site
Mount Ida 12880 ft
Mount Julian 12928ft
36
Beaver Meadows Visitor Center
Estes Park
Lake Estes

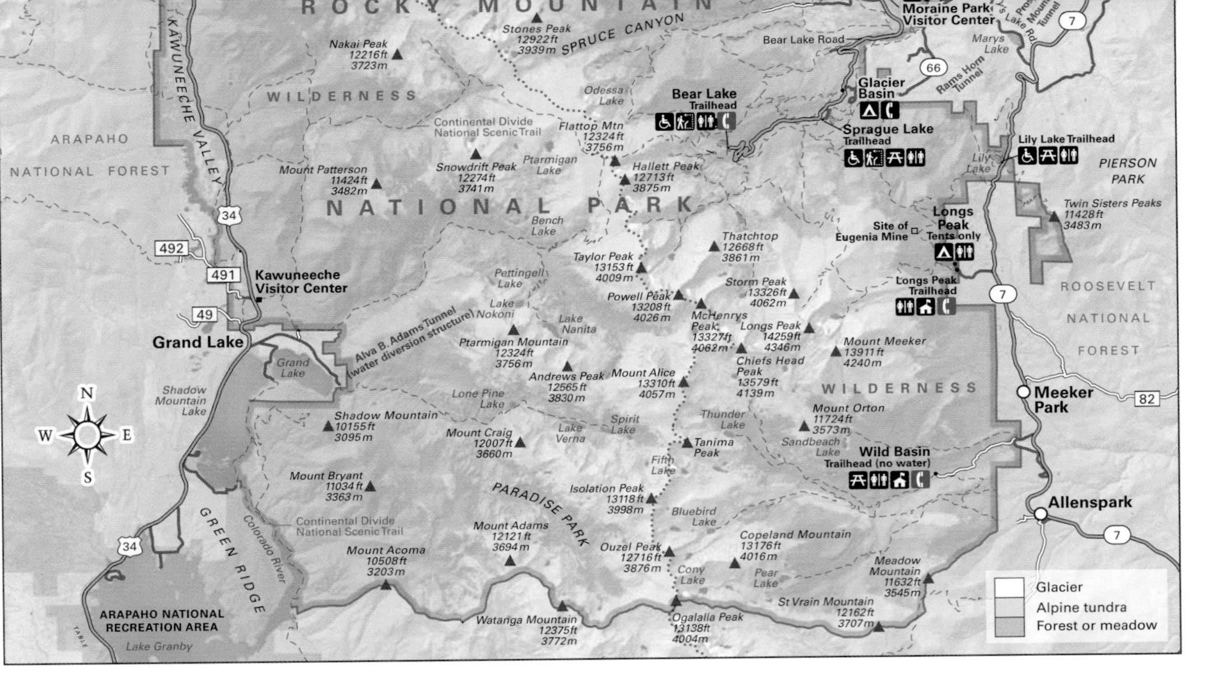
ROCKY MOUNTAIN NATIONAL PARK
Moraine Park Visitor Center
Bear Lake Road
Marys Lake
Rams Horn Tunnel
66
7
Glacier Basin
Bear Lake Trailhead
Sprague Lake Trailhead
Lily Lake Trailhead
Lily Lake
PIERSON PARK
Twin Sisters Peaks 11428 ft 3483 m
Longs Peak Tents only
Site of Eugenia Mine
Longs Peak Trailhead
ROOSEVELT NATIONAL FOREST
Meeker Park
82
Allenspark
WILDERNESS
Stones Peak 12922 ft 3939 m
SPRUCE CANYON
Nakai Peak 12216 ft 3723 m
Odessa Lake
Continental Divide National Scenic Trail
Flattop Mtn 12324 ft 3756 m
Hallett Peak 12713 ft 3875 m
Ptarmigan Lake
Snowdrift Peak 12274 ft 3741 m
Mount Patterson 11424 ft 3482 m
ARAPAHO NATIONAL FOREST
KAWUNEECHE VALLEY
34
492
491
49
Kawuneeche Visitor Center
Grand Lake
Bench Lake
Thatchtop 12668 ft 3861 m
Taylor Peak 13153 ft 4009 m
Pettingell Lake
Storm Peak 13326 ft 4062 m
Powell Peak 13208 ft 4026 m
McHenrys Peak 13327 ft 4062 m
Longs Peak 14259 ft 4346 m
Mount Meeker 13911 ft 4240 m
Lake Nokoni
Lake Nanita
Alva B. Adams Tunnel (water diversion structure)
Ptarmigan Mountain 12324 ft 3756 m
Chiefs Head Peak 13579 ft 4139 m
Andrews Peak 12565 ft 3830 m
Mount Alice 13310 ft 4057 m
Shadow Mountain Lake
Lone Pine Lake
Shadow Mountain 10155 ft 3095 m
Spirit Lake
Thunder Lake
Mount Orton 11724 ft 3573 m
Mount Craig 12007 ft 3660 m
Lake Verna
Tanima Peak
Sandbeach Lake
Wild Basin Trailhead (no water)
Fifth Lake
Mount Bryant 11034 ft 3363 m
PARADISE PARK
Isolation Peak 13118 ft 3998 m
Bluebird Lake
GREEN RIDGE
Colorado River
Mount Adams 12121 ft 3694 m
Copeland Mountain 13176 ft 4016 m
Ouzel Peak 12716 ft 3876 m
Meadow Mountain 11632 ft 3545 m
Mount Acoma 10508 ft 3203 m
Cony Lake
Pear Lake
St Vrain Mountain 12162 ft 3707 m
ARAPAHO NATIONAL RECREATION AREA
Lake Granby
Watanga Mountain 12375 ft 3772 m
Ogalalla Peak 13138 ft 4004 m
N
E
S
W
Glacier
Alpine tundra
Forest or meadow

Acknowledgments

Many thanks to the faithful park personnel of Rocky Mountain National Park who have dedicated their lives to preserving the natural resources of the park and sharing the natural wonders of "Rocky" with visitors. We would especially like to thank Larry Frederick, Jeff Conner, Scott Roederer, Tim Burchett, and Scott Rashid for sharing their wealth of knowledge about the park's natural history. Our thanks also go to Curt Buchholtz, Megan Matzen, and the staff and members of the Rocky Mountain Nature Association for their continued support of the interpretative and educational mission of the park. Special thanks go to Becky Gregory for her special contributions to this book. We would also like to thank all the staff at Globe Pequot's FalconGuides, especially Jessica Haberman, whose support and efforts made this National Park Nature Guide series a reality. We would like to thank our family for their love and support.

Finally, we would like to dedicate this book to Nick Prillaman Jr. and Herb Petty, two men whose lives reminded us to seek delight in simple pleasures and to enjoy, share, and preserve that which we love.

Rocky Mountain Nature Association

The Rocky Mountain Nature Association, Inc. (RMNA) promotes the understanding of Rocky Mountain National Park and similar public lands through interpretive and educational publications and programs; advances stewardship through philanthropy for Rocky Mountain National Park and similar public lands; protects, restores, maintains and preserves land and historic sites in Rocky Mountain National Park and in the Rocky Mountain West; and may, in furtherance of such mission, conduct any lawful activity. Visit us at www.rmna.org.

Rocky Mountain National Park established in 1915

Introduction

When Enos Mills first stepped atop Longs Peak, he knew that the sweeping vistas stretching before him were incomparable to any he had ever seen. Nearly one hundred years later, we can enjoy this singular, magnificent area too, thanks to the conservation efforts of men like Enos Mills, James Grafton Rogers, and others who lobbied to protect this extraordinary land. As a result of their vision and commitment, President Woodrow Wilson signed a bill in 1915 establishing Rocky Mountain National Park as our nation's tenth national park.

Enos Mills, early champion of park conservation.
IMAGE COURTESY OF ROCKY MOUNTAIN NATIONAL PARK

Nature Guide to Rocky Mountain National Park was written as an easy-to-use guide for those who've come to visit this natural wonder, or who may be contemplating a trip. Sized to fit in a pocket, it identifies some of the most common plants, animals, and natural features of the park. Technical terms have been kept to a minimum, and a color picture accompanies each description. Entries often include natural history notes and ethnobotanical and/or historical remarks.

We care for the things that we know and so hope this introduction to the nature of the park will spark an interest in the natural world and generate further interest in care for, and support of, the environment.

About Rocky Mountain National Park

Soaring snowcapped peaks, plunging waterfalls, and high mountain lakes amplify the rugged beauty and grandeur of the southern Rockies set aside as Rocky Mountain National Park. About ninety minutes north of Denver, "Rocky" is one of the top-ten visited national parks. A top wildlife-watching destination, the park

Longs Peak glows in the sunrise.

Longs Peak overlooks the changing autumn leaves of Aspen.

attracts more than three million visitors each year, who come to see bighorn sheep, mule deer, moose, black bears, and especially the great herds of elk. Plants are an attraction too. Elevations that range from 7,640 to 14,259 feet at Longs Peak create a wide diversity of habitats for over 1,000 plant species. The park's unique habitats and features have been set aside as an International Biosphere Reserve. With over 280 species of birds, the park has also been designated a Globally Important Bird Area.

One of the best ways to explore the park is Trail Ridge Road. Climbing from elevations of about 8,000 feet to over 12,000 feet into the alpine tundra, this is the highest continuous paved highway in the United States. Designated a National Scenic Byway, it offers breathtaking vistas that course over layers of snowcapped mountaintops and provides easy access to the unique environment and ecosystem of one of the most endangered habitats in the world, the fragile alpine tundra.

Dividing the park is the mountainous spine called the Continental Divide. Water flowing from the east side eventually flows into the Atlantic Ocean, while streams on the west flow to the Pacific. Estes Park is Rocky's eastern gateway, where visitors can find lodging, food, and other supplies. On the west side, the small community of Grand Lake offers visitor services. Trail Ridge Road connects the west side to the east, but weather conditions close the road in winter, and an alternate route around the park must be taken.

Arriving from the Denver area or other easterly locations, most visitors enter at the Beaver Meadows Entrance Station, which is 3.5 miles west of Estes Park on US 36 or the Fall River Entrance Station on US 34, four miles west of Estes Park. About 19 miles south of Estes Park on CO 7, visitors can enter the park at the Wild Basin Entrance station.

Visitors entering from the west pass through the Grand Lake Entrance Station about 2 miles north of Grand Lake. Popular shuttle buses are available in summer months from Beaver Meadows Visitor Center to Bear Lake and Moraine Park.

Although the park is open every day of the year, visitor services vary seasonally. Visitor centers on the east side include Beaver Meadows, Fall River, Moraine Park, and Alpine. The Sheep Lakes Information Station is open usually beginning in May. The west side is served by the Kawuneeche Visitor Center.

It is highly recommended that you begin your visit with a stop at one of these visitor centers, where you can learn about park activities such as the Junior Ranger programs or activities sponsored by the Rocky Mountain Nature Association. These programs can make a nice addition to other popular park activities, such as picnicking, hiking, rock climbing, fishing, horseback riding, bird watching, and butterfly and dragonfly watching. Popular winter activities include sledding, snowshoeing, and cross-country skiing. Or you may want to just see how many animals you can find. Year-round, wildlife viewing is the number-one activity of visitors to the park. Many people enjoy simply driving through the park to enjoy the spectacular scenery. You can check road conditions by calling the park's information office at (970) 586-1206 or visiting www.nps.gov/romo.

If you plan to camp, your choices include Aspenglen, Glacier Basin, Longs Peak, Moraine Park, and Timber Creek.

Park conservation is encouraged in the Junior Ranger Program.

Safety Notes

Always let someone know when you go for a hike. Dress in layers and carry raingear and plenty of water, as weather conditions can change rapidly. Hypothermia can occur at any time of year, so carry warm clothing. Lightning is a severe threat in the park, especially above tree line in the afternoons. Try to begin hikes early in the day, but if you're caught by a fast-moving storm, stay away from summits and isolated trees and rocks. Crouch down on your heels. Be aware of avalanche threats, thin ice, and rapid streams. Be aware of falling trees and branches, especially when hiking in beetle-infested areas in the park. The dead trees present hazardous conditions, including falling limbs and fire hazards. Park officials are addressing this enormous task by removing hazardous trees in high-impact areas and by prescribed burns. Thin air at high elevations increases the chance of mountain sickness;

symptoms include headaches, nausea, and dizziness. If you experience mountain sickness, move to a lower elevation (see Elevations of Common Park Destinations on page xx). Dehydration and severe sunburn can be prevented by drinking plenty of water and applying sunscreen.

Never feed wildlife. Not only is it illegal, but it endangers the welfare of the animal. Food and trash must be stored properly to avoid attracting wildlife. The park provides bear boxes near popular trailheads. Backcountry campers must provide their own bear-proof food canisters or containers for this purpose. When hiking, stay a safe distance from wildlife. While you don't need to be aware of grizzly bears or poisonous snakes as they are not found in the park, there are mountain lions and black bears. Make noise while you're hiking so they can avoid you, don't hike alone, and if attacked, fight back. Never let small children run ahead of you on trails. Keep them beside you and pick them up if a bear or lion is encountered. Stop, do not run, speak in a firm, calm voice, and try to appear larger.

Ticks are common throughout the park, so take precautions to prevent bites that may result in Colorado tick fever or Rocky Mountain spotted fever. To avoid tick bites, tuck your pants into your socks and wear long-sleeved shirts. Walk on the center of trails rather than taking shortcuts through the brush. Use insect repellant and do "tick checks" especially on the hairline, waistline, and groin areas. Avoid removing ticks with your bare hands; instead, use tweezers and protect your fingers with a tissue. Grasp the tick as close to the skin as possible and pull upward with a steady even pressure. Jerking or twisting can cause the mouthparts to break off in the skin. If this happens, either remove the mouthparts with tweezers or leave it alone and allow the skin to heal. Wash the area and your hands thoroughly. Avoid folklore treatments such as burning the tick or trying to smother it with nail polish or petroleum jelly. If within a week you develop flulike symptoms or a rash, see your health care provider. While these diseases are easily treated with antibiotics, they can become very severe or even fatal without treatment.

Proper food storage is important to protect you and wildlife.

Conservation Note

Please leave wildflowers where they grow. When hiking, stay on established trails and watch where you put your feet to avoid damaging plants. In Rocky Mountain National Park it is illegal to pick, dig, or damage any plant including mushrooms. Please report any suspicious activity to a park ranger.

How to Use This Guide

Common and Scientific Name

Common names of plants and animals are prominently given in each entry. Since these sometimes vary by locality, each organism's unique Latin name, composed of genus and species, is also presented. Additionally, common names of families are included in each entry. Genetic research is rapidly discovering new inherent relationships and associations; therefore, the taxonomic status of many organisms listed has changed from previous publications.

Photo Tips

Sharp focus is the key to taking great nature photos. Overcast days offer nice soft lighting for wildflowers and animals. In deep shade, increase the ISO or use a flash. Bright sunny days create harsh shadows and a flash is needed to add detail to the shaded areas of a flower or to add a speck of light to the eye. If your camera or lens has image stabilization capability, you can use it to help stop motion. Shooting close-ups at f16 with a flash will give more depth of field and stop motion. When taking wildflower photos, be careful not to trample other plants. Use a telephoto lens to zoom in on wildlife, and keep the eye in focus. Never approach too closely just to get a picture. If your behavior changes the behavior of the animal, you are too close. A tripod is necessary for low lighting conditions in the early morning or evening.

Suggested Nature Hikes and Wildlife Viewing Areas

The following areas or trails are suggested for the general public and families who want to see wildlife, wildflowers, and other natural features of Rocky Mountain National Park. Some of the recommended trails are wheelchair accessible or accessible with assistance. Of course, the wild animals and plants of the park may not always be where expected, so it is a good idea to first stop at

Cyclists enjoy fall splendor on Old Fall River Road.

a visitor center and check with a park ranger about recent sightings. To find other attractive hikes, consult a topographic map or hiking guides such as Kent and Donna Dannen's *Best Easy Day Hikes* and *Hiking Rocky Mountain National Park* (FalconGuides). These and other interpretive publications are offered in the visitor center bookstores operated by Rocky Mountain Nature Association. Remember to maintain a safe distance from wildlife and never feed wildlife. Please do not pick any wildflowers or mushrooms or remove any natural objects from the park. Remember, you're more likely to see wild animals during the early morning and evening when they're more active.

1. Trail Ridge Road. You can travel the 48 miles between Estes Park and Grand Lake into the alpine tundra along this National Scenic Byway. Closed in winter, the road climbs to an elevation of 12,183 feet. Elk and bighorn sheep graze the lush alpine meadows. If you can take your eyes off the spectacular views at overlooks such as Forest Canyon Overlook, you can enjoy vibrant alpine wildflower displays. At Rainbow Curve, it is easy to spot chipmunks, golden-mantled ground squirrels, gray jays, and Clark's nutcrackers. At Rock Cut, the Tundra Communities Trail is paved but steep. Alpine wildflowers line the trail, and hikers can watch for marmots and pikas that sun themselves on the boulders near the trailhead. Stop at Lava Cliffs to look for brown-capped rosy-finches, prairie falcons, ravens, American pipits and horned larks. Patient butterfly watchers may be rewarded with views of high altitude butterfly specialties such as Melissa arctic and Magdalena alpines. One of the best places to search for ptarmigan is Medicine Bow Curve.

2. Sheep Lakes. A parking area provides views into the meadows around Sheep Lakes. This is a great place to see bighorn sheep, elk, coyotes, and mountain bluebirds. In spring, bighorn sheep cross the road to feed on the minerals around the lake. In warm months, listen for the raspy comblike call of boreal chorus frogs.

ELEVATIONS OF COMMON PARK DESTINATIONS

Destination	Elevation (ft)
Estes Park (Downtown)	7,522
Beaver Meadows Visitor Center	7,840
Moraine Park Visitor Center	8,140
Moraine Park Campground	8,160
Aspenglen Campground	8,200
Fall River Visitor Center	8,250
Grand Lake (Town)	8,367
Wild Basin Entrance	8,390
Glacier Basin Campground	8,500
Kawuneeche Visitor Center	8,720
Timber Creek Campground	8,900
Hidden Valley	9,240
Bear Lake	9,475
Longs Peak Campground	9,500
Many Parks Curve	9,640
Milner Pass / Poudre Lake	10,758
Rainbow Curve	10,829
Medicine Bow Overlook	11,660
Forest Canyon Overlook	11,716
Alpine Visitor Center	11,796
Lava Cliffs Parking Area	12,000
Rock Cut	12,050

3. Bear Lake. Take the park shuttle bus to enjoy the subalpine lakes and trails near Bear Lake. A 1-mile hike from Bear Lake parking area brings you to Nymph Lake at 9,700 feet. Slightly 1 more mile beyond you will reach Dream Lake at 9,000 feet. Along the way, watch for snowshoe hares, pine martens and woodland wildflowers. In winter, you can join a ranger for a snowshoe hike around the lake (check at the visitor center for this and other winter activities).

4. Kawuneeche Valley. The west side of the park offers the best opportunity to see moose browsing amid the willow thickets and wet meadows. Coyote Valley Trail is a 1-mile wheelchair-accessible trail that follows the Colorado River into Kawuneeche Valley. Bring your binoculars and watch for moose, elk, and red-tailed hawks flying over the meadow. Along the 1-mile round-trip gravel path to the Holzwarth Historic Site, watch for birds such as red-naped sapsucker, Cordilleran flycatcher, western wood peewee, and broad-tailed hummingbird.

5. Old Fall River Road. Open only in summer, Old Fall River Road is a one-way, winding gravel road that provides spectacular views into the park. Look for black bears, butterflies, wildflowers, and boreal forest birds such as blue grouse, mountain chickadees, and yellow-rumped warblers. Elk, mule deer, and bighorn sheep may be spotted along the way. Spectacular hillside displays of Indian paintbrush, mountain harebell, fireweed, waxflower, and stately cow parsnip line the road.

6. Wild Basin / Copeland Falls / Calypso Cascades. In Wild Basin you will find abundant wildflowers such as fairy slipper orchids, pinedrops, and chiming bells. Along the trail watch for playful chipmunks, golden-mantled ground squirrels, and red squirrels. See if you can spot water ouzels diving into the cold mountain stream for insects.

7. Endovalley. The Alluvial Fan picnic area is one of the best spots in the park for bird watching as many species use the area trees and thickets as nest sites. Up to four species of birds may cavity nest in one aspen tree. This is a great place to watch birds, including woodpeckers, house wrens, nesting tree swallows, black-billed magpies, pygmy nuthatches, Lincoln's sparrows and great horned owls. Look for long-tailed weasel, coyotes, and golden-mantled ground squirrels. In fall, colorful aspens light up this and other areas of Horseshoe Park.

8. Lily Lake. The three-quarter-mile fully wheelchair-accessible gravel trail that surrounds Lily Lake is a great place to spot the endangered greenback cutthroat trout. Waterfowl such as ring-neck ducks and mallards feed along the calm lake edges. Red-winged blackbirds nest in the tall wetland plants. Slow down and watch for colorful butterflies and dragonflies along the wetland edges. Pasqueflowers and other spring wildflowers bloom along the trail.

Bighorn sheep congregate in the fertile meadows of Rocky Mountain National Park.

Please drive slowly to protect wildlife.

9. Moraine Park. The last two weeks in September find the park packed with visitors to watch the exciting fall elk action. At the peak of the rut, bull elk vie for females with loud bugling and intense fighting. The loud clash of antlers can be heard as visitors watch and take photos from a safe distance. The "show" usually begins just before sunset. Some trails are closed during this time, and park rangers and trained volunteers are on hand to help keep visitors at a safe distance.

10. Sprague Lake. A half mile of wheelchair-accessible gravel trail encircles picturesque Sprague Lake. Muskrats slip under the wetland boardwalk and Wilson's warblers greet visitors from the thickets. Mallard ducklings follow their protective mothers in the area near the picnic grounds. American beavers busily tend their lodges in the wetland areas.

Lush riparian wetlands provide excellent habitat for wildlife in the montane zone.

Ecosystems

The soaring peaks of the Continental Divide cut Rocky Mountain National Park in two and provide the spectacular scenery for which the park is world-renowned. From Big Thompson River at 7,640 feet to Longs Peak at 14,250 feet, more than sixty peaks tower above 12,000 feet, creating a living model of biological diversity in an area encompassing only about 415 square miles. Three separate ecosystems flourish here: montane, subalpine, and alpine.

Occurring between 5,600 and 9,500 feet, the montane ecosystem is characterized by ponderosa pine, Douglas-fir, lodgepole pine and quaking aspen. Areas called riparian zones where streams or rivers course through the montane forests are important habitat for wildlife providing water, food, and shelter.

Going upslope, the subalpine ecosystem follows, beginning about 9,000 feet and rising to 11,000 feet. Here the landscape is dominated by tall, straight Engelmann spruce and subalpine fir. Approaching the upper elevations, environmental conditions worsen as strong winds kill the lateral buds on their windward

Plants and animals that live in the alpine tundra face harsh weather conditions.

side, leaving "banner" or "flag" trees with growth on one side only. Pushing the limits of existence, only the hardiest trees can withstand conditions near elevations of 11,000 feet. Harsh wind conditions create deformed, stunted trees in a dense, low growth form called *krummholz* which is German for "twisted wood."

From 11,000 to 11,500 feet, the wind speeds of the alpine ecosystem may reach over 200 miles per hour. With extreme cold temperatures and harsh conditions, trees are not able to survive, but dwarfed willow shrubs may grow in semisheltered areas. Amazingly, tiny flowers that keep low to the ground are able to exist here by blooming fast in the short growing season. These plants have long roots for support and dense hairs or waxy surfaces to provide protection from the drying winds. Special pigments protect the flowers from the intense ultraviolet radiation at this high altitude. About one third of Rocky Mountain National Park is composed of this fragile ecosystem, and Trail Ridge Road provides an extraordinary opportunity for visitors to experience this unique ecosystem.

Alpine Visitor Center was built on the edge of a cirque, the remnant of a giant glacier that filled the Fall River Valley.

Geology

The geologic story of the park is visible in the sixty peaks over 12,000 feet, U-shaped valleys carved by glaciers, the remains of violent volcanic activity, and metamorphic rocks whose origins date back to vast inland seas that predate life on earth. Over millions of years the mountains were formed, creating the schist, gneiss, and granite that make up most of the park's rocks.

A few glaciers remain in the park, and bowl-shaped cirques (rhymes with "works") cap the top of valleys formed by glaciers. When the glaciers finally melted, the masses of rock (glacial till) that they displaced were left behind in long, large ridges called moraines.

In Horseshoe Park, the Alluvial Fan was formed when the Lawn Lake Dam failed on July 15, 1982, releasing a torrent of water from the Roaring Fork River into the valley. The remaining boulders and unconsolidated materials spread out in a fan shaped area called an alluvial fan. Alluvial comes from the Latin word *alluere,* which means "to wash against."

BIGHORN SHEEP

Ovis canadensis

Cattle family (Bovidae)

Quick ID: gray-brown coat with white rump patch, about 3' tall at shoulder, horns

Length: 5–6' Weight: 120–340 lb

The official Colorado state animal is found in Rocky Mountain National Park: About 600 bighorn or mountain sheep call the park home. Agile climbers, bighorn sheep find security from predators on rocky ledges. The horns of male bighorn sheep weighing up to thirty pounds, grow throughout their lives, and are not shed. Males, or "rams," use their curled massive horns in head-butting displays to win mating rights. The horns of females or "ewes" grow in a spike about 8 inches tall. In spring, lambs are born in protected areas of the high country. In late spring and early summer, the sheep descend into Sheep Lakes in Horseshoe Park to make use of the high mineral content of the soil.

COYOTE

Canis latrans

Dog family (Canidae)

Quick ID: medium size, doglike; gray to reddish coat

Length: 2.5–3.3'   Weight: 15–44 lb

About the size of a small German shepherd, the coyote has long been considered one of the most intelligent members of the animal kingdom. Sometimes despised as problem animals, coyotes are extremely versatile and are able to quickly adjust to a wide variety of habitats and circumstances. Preying on rodents, rabbits, squirrels, and insects, coyotes will supplement their omnivorous diet with fruit, plants, and carrion. Coyotes sometimes hunt in pairs, displaying the complex thought patterns of skilled hunters as they stalk their prey. Mated pairs often remain together for years. Look for coyotes throughout the park, especially around Sheep Lakes and Moraine Park.

RED FOX

Vulpes vulpes

Dog family (Canidae)

Quick ID: small, doglike; reddish coat, white underneath; white-tipped, bushy tail

Length: 2.7–3.6' Weight: 7–15 lb

Weighing less than a cocker spaniel, the red fox sometimes looks larger than it really is due to its luxurious orange-red coat. In winter, the fox wraps its 15-inch bushy, white-tipped tail around its face for added warmth. This white-tipped tail is a good way to distinguish the red fox from the coyote, which competes with the fox for food sources. An omnivore, the fox will eat rodents and other small mammals as well as berries, insects, earthworms, nuts, and carrion. Very shy and primarily nocturnal, the red fox is not commonly seen in the park. Dawn and dusk are the best times to see a fox, especially in the park's lower-altitude meadows.

AMERICAN BEAVER

Castor canadensis

Beaver family (Castoridae)

Quick ID: dark brown; broad, flat tail

Length: 3–3.9' Weight: 35–66 lb

Widely recognized by its large, flat, paddle-shaped tail, the American beaver is an important inhabitant of Rocky Mountain National Park. Wide oversized front teeth enable beavers to gnaw down trees which they use to build dams and lodges in streams. Adept at conserving oxygen, these aquatic specialists can remain submerged for fifteen minutes. Areas of the park that owe their development to the industrious work of generations of beavers include Horseshoe Park and Beaver Meadows. In addition to these areas, you may be able to spot beavers in Sprague Lake and other areas with sufficient willows, which beavers use as winter food. Competition with increasing elk use of willows may contribute to the decrease in the numbers of the park's beavers.

ELK

Cervus elaphus

Deer family (Cervidae)

Quick ID: larger than mule deer but smaller than moose, brown with large cream-colored rump patch, tail without black tip

Length: 6.5–8.5' Weight: 400–1,100 lb

Shrill resonating bugles pierce the crisp fall air during the fall elk rut in Rocky Mountain National Park. Standing up to 5 feet at the shoulder, bull elk have large antlers made of bone. Weighing up to forty pounds, the antlers are shed each year in spring. Female elk, called cows, do not have antlers. The common name *wapiti* is derived from the Shawnee word for "white rump." Most active at dawn and dusk, elk can be seen in large herds in autumn in Moraine Park, Upper Beaver Meadows, Horseshoe Park, and Kawuneeche Valley. In summer, they may be seen grazing the lush alpine meadows with their newborn calves, but with the arrival of winter, most elk move into the sheltered valleys surrounding the park.

MOOSE

Alces alces

Deer family (Cervidae)

Quick ID: dark brown, larger than elk or mule deer, horselike nose

Length: 8–10' Weight: 600–1,600 lb

A majestic symbol of wilderness, bull moose sport large, flattened antlers through fall but shed them in early spring. The antlers may span 6 feet across and weigh up to seventy pounds. Females, called cows, never grow antlers and are smaller than males. Reaching up to 7 feet tall at the shoulder, moose are unpredictable and can run at speeds of up to 35 miles per hour. Use binoculars or a spotting scope to observe moose from a distance. The best place to spot moose in the park is in the willow thickets and wetlands of the Kawuneeche Valley where they graze on sodium-rich aquatic vegetation.

MULE DEER

Odocoileus hemionus

Deer family (Cervidae)

Quick ID: grayish brown to red brown, white rump patch, black-tipped tail

Length: 4.1–5.5' Weight: 66–264 lb

Aptly named, mule deer sport ears that are abnormally large and resemble those of a mule. They also have distinctive black-tipped tails. Sometimes called black-tailed deer or "mulies," these deer are usually found throughout the park at lower elevations than those frequented by their larger elk relatives. The antlers of bucks branch into two separate tines; females do not have antlers. When startled or nervous, mule deer perform an interesting hop called "stotting," in which the deer bounds repeatedly into the air and all four feet hit the ground at the same time. Mule deer can be spotted along the Old Fall River Road, Endovalley, and in the Kawuneeche Valley area.

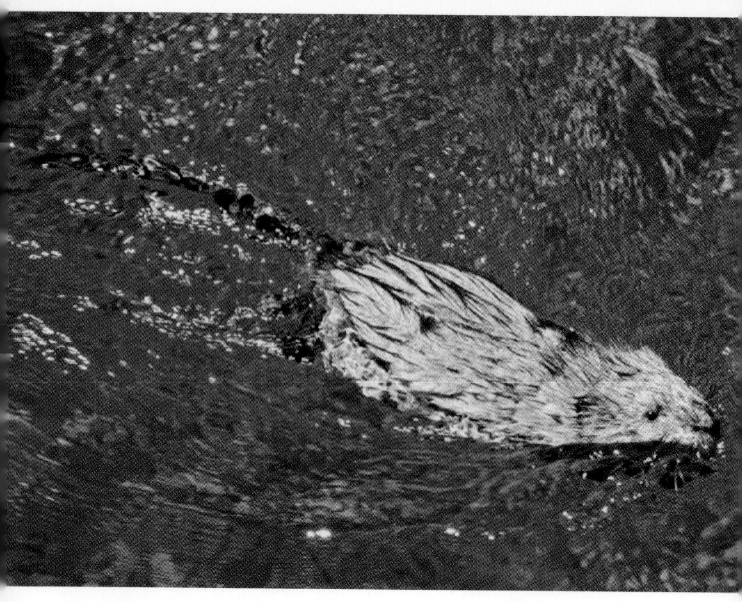

MUSKRAT

Ondatra zibethicus

Mice, rat, and vole family (Cricetidae)

Quick ID: brown, laterally flattened tail, aquatic

Length: 16"–2'   Weight: 1.5–3.9 lb

Experts at life in a marsh, muskrats are equipped with waterproof fur and webbed feet. They either build tunnel burrows in mud banks or domed lodges made of piles of soft vegetation. Even though muskrats are similar in appearance and habitat to beavers, they are much smaller, weigh much less, and have a long, narrow tail rather than the flattened paddle-like tail of the beaver. Biologists describe muskrats as mainly crepuscular, a term used to describe animals that are most active at dawn and dusk. At Sprague Lake, muskrats can often be spotted swimming by the boardwalk trail.

NORTH AMERICAN PORCUPINE

Erethizon dorsatum

Porcupine family (Erethizontidae)

Quick ID: brown, chunky body, arching back, yellowish quills

Length: 2–4.3' Weight: 7.7–39.6 lb

In a unique example of survival in the natural world, the hairs of the North American porcupine have evolved into an exceptional defense system. This slow-moving woodland inhabitant has a soft underbelly but defends itself with 30,000 barbed quills on its back and short tail. The waxy quills are tipped with tiny barbs that inflict a painful stab to the attacker. Once embedded, the quills are designed to work their way downward and if they do not hit vital organs may eventually exit from the other side. Contrary to popular myth, porcupines cannot throw their quills but they detach readily when brushed up against a solid object. Nocturnal animals, porcupines spend the day sleeping in tall trees throughout the park.

BOBCAT

Lynx rufus

Cat family (Felidae)

Quick ID: tawny to gray with black spots and bars, ear tufts, short tail

Length: 18"–4' Weight: 8.4–68 lb

Often called wildcats, bobcats are about twice as large as a house cat with a short bobbed tail. Spotted all over and with small black ear tufts, bobcats are smaller than lynx, which have also been recently found in the park. The tip of a lynx's tail is entirely black, while the tip of a bobcat's tail is black on top with white underneath. Bobcats are widespread but are not typically seen as they usually hunt at night preying on small mammals such as rabbits and rodents. Solitary animals, bobcats often spend their days resting on rocky outcrops, or in hollow logs or dense brush.

MOUNTAIN LION

Puma concolor

Cat family (Felidae)

Quick ID: tawny brown uniform color with no spots (except as young), very long tail

Length: 5–9'   Weight: 75–230 lb

Once widespread throughout the country, the mountain lion or cougar has reclaimed its domain in many areas of the west, including the rugged mountains of Rocky Mountain National Park. Powerful predators at the top of the food chain, their success depends on an abundance of prey and plenty of appropriate habitat. Deer, elk, and a variety of smaller mammals are sources of prey. Approaching the height of a Great Dane but with a stockier body, a cougar normally avoids human contact; however, as people encroach on wild habitat, encounters are inevitable. Avoid hiking alone, keep pets on a leash, and absolutely never let children run ahead of you on trails. If attacked, fight back.

NORTHERN POCKET GOPHER

Thomomys talpoides

Pocket gopher family (Geomyidae)

Quick ID: Large, brownish, mouselike, big claws, large front teeth

Length: 6–10.5" Weight: 2–5.5 oz

Rarely seen, this rodent lives in underground tunnels dug with its continuously growing teeth and sharp thick claws. It may pull plants underground to eat them. In winter, it lines snow tunnels with dirt which, when the snow melts, are left as sinuous earthen ridges known as pocket gopher "eskers."

MOUNTAIN COTTONTAIL

Sylvilagus nuttallii

Rabbit and hare family (Leporidae)

Quick ID: small, pale, gray-brown rabbit; black-tipped ears

Length: 13.3–15.3" Weight: 1.4–1.9 lb

Also known as Nuttall's cottontail, the mountain cottontail is one of three rabbit and hare species found in the park. This small rabbit is found in woody or brushy areas of the park. The genus, *Sylvilagus,* means "rabbit of the forest," and the species name, *nuttallii,* was given to this rabbit to honor Thomas Nuttall, a botanist and naturalist explorer of the early 1800s. Rabbits, like the mountain cottontail, are born hairless with their eyes closed and must be cared for by their mother for several weeks. Predators of these rabbits include bobcats, coyotes, and raptors such as red-tail hawks and owls.

SNOWSHOE HARE

Lepus americanus

Rabbit and hare family (Leporidae)

Quick ID: medium-size brown rabbit, white in winter, moderately long black-tipped ears, large hind feet

Length: 14.3–20.4" Weight: 2–4.8 lb

Snowshoe hares have earned the common name "bigfoot" for a great reason—they have very long hind feet and toes padded with thick hair that allows them to travel easily on top of the snow. Hares such as the snowshoe hare and the larger white-tailed jackrabbit, *L. townsendii,* are born with fur and can eat grass within hours of birth. Primarily nocturnal, the snowshoe hare is best spotted around dawn or dusk. In winter, look for tracks in the snow near Bear Lake. Due to their hopping movements, the hind footprint is in front of the front footprint.

STRIPED SKUNK

Mephitis mephitis

Skunk family (Mephitidae)

Quick ID: black, 2 broad white stripes along back, large bushy tail

Length: 20"–2.3' Weight: 6–14 lb

Sporting two white racing stripes, this widely recognized mammal hardly needs an introduction. About the size of a large house cat, the striped skunk is joined in the park by the smaller western spotted skunk, *Spilogale gracilis.* Skunks are omnivores, eating a wide variety of foods including insects, small rodents, and berries. Skunks represented healing to the Arapaho, who used skunk oil from the scent glands to treat earaches. The odious spray of a skunk was treated by looking directly into an old pair of smelly moccasins.

AMERICAN BADGER

Taxidea taxus

Weasel family (Mustelidae)

Quick ID: flat heavy body, short legs, white median stripe on head

Length: 2–2.6' Weight: 8–26 lb

If you happen to spot a waddling, short-legged, shaggy animal the height of a medium-size dog, you may have just spied an American badger. A badger's body is covered with grizzled-gray coarse hair, but its face is quite distinctive, with blackish patches on white cheeks. A white stripe begins at its nose and continues onto its head and shoulders. The forelimbs and claws of badgers are adept at digging, which is how they catch most of their food, tunneling after underground rodents and other prey. Mostly nocturnal, badgers may sometimes be spotted heading into their burrows or even culverts under the road near Moraine Park.

AMERICAN MARTEN

Martes americana

Weasel family (Mustelidae)

Quick ID: yellowish brown fur, bushy tail, catlike ears

Length: 1.5–2.2' Weight: 1.5–2.5 lb

Often called pine marten, the American marten is a member of the weasel family. A tree lover, this agile climber can even come down trees head first, arching its long body inchworm fashion. The similar mink has a white patch on its chin. Mostly nocturnal, the marten feeds on small mammals such as chickarees and voles but will also eat insects, fruit, and nuts. Look for these delightful mammals in the tops of tall trees in Kawuneeche Valley and Bear Lake.

ERMINE

Mustela erminea

Weasel family (Mustelidae)

Quick ID: brown with whitish belly, white feet, turns white in winter, black-tipped tail

Length: 7.5–13.5"   Weight: 1–4 oz

The secretive ermine, or short-tailed weasel, is not commonly seen in the park. Sometime called a "stoat," this small animal has soft, fine, light brown fur and a creamy white belly and throat. In winter, its coat is totally white except for the persistent black tip on the tail. These seasonal cryptic color changes allow the ermine to use camouflage to capture prey more easily as these voracious predators need to eat constantly to maintain their high metabolic rate. Look for ermine in rocky areas of the high country and along tundra trails near Alpine Visitor Center.

LONG-TAILED WEASEL

Mustela frenata

Weasel family (Mustelidae)

Quick ID: brown back and sides, yellowish belly, brownish feet, turns white in winter, black-tipped tail

Length: 11–16.5" Weight: 3.2 oz–1 lb

Moving quickly along logs or under shrubs with bounding, arched movements, the long-tailed weasel catches the eye of visitors lucky to enough to get a glimpse. Its identifying characteristics are its long sinuous brown body, long neck, and rounded ears atop a triangular head. Sometimes confused with the ermine or short-tailed weasel, the long-tailed weasel is aptly named, as its 3- to 6-inch-long black-tipped tail is often a third as long as its body. Molting in fall produces white cryptic fur that blends well with the snowy environment. Keep an eye out for long-tailed weasels in picnic areas in Endovalley.

NORTH AMERICAN RIVER OTTER

Lontra canadensis

Weasel family (Mustelidae)

Quick ID: rich, brown fur; long, round tail; webbed feet

Length: 2.9–4.3' Weight: 11–30 lb

Much larger than the more common muskrat, the North American river otter can be found in the west side of the park in and along the Colorado River in Kawuneeche Valley. Its streamlined body and 12- to 18-inch tail, which is used like a rudder, allow the river otter to swim rapidly and capture fish with ease. Its dense, soft fur protects and insulates the animal from cold, but has also been an attraction for trappers. By the early 1900s, over-trapping for pelts caused a decline in river otter numbers, but reintroduction programs have helped maintain populations.

AMERICAN PIKA

Ochotona princeps

Pika family (Ochotonidae)

Quick ID: grayish brown, resembles a guinea pig, found in talus rock areas

Length: 6.5–8.5" Weight: 4–6.5 oz

You will probably hear its territorial high-pitched, single "bleet" call before you see this tiny rock climber that lives only at high elevations amidst boulder fields. With its small rounded ears and soft gray-brown fur, the American pika somewhat resembles a guinea pig but is actually more closely related to rabbits. During summer days, pikas busily gather vegetation to store in hay piles for the long winter. These hardy alpine specialists require cool temperatures to exist. The alpine tundra protected by Rocky Mountain National Park is vital to their existence especially as the effects of global warming threaten its fragile habitat. Pronounced "pie-ka" or sometimes "pee-ka," you can look for pikas along Trail Ridge Road especially at Rock Cut area.

NORTHERN RACCOON

Procyon lotor

Raccoon family (Procyonidae)

Quick ID: gray, black facial mask, black rings on tail

Length: 2–3.1' Weight: 4–22 lb

The masked joker of the night, raccoons are nocturnal and rarely seen during the daytime. Omnivores, they eat a wide variety of foods, including insects, plants, small mammals, fruit, and nuts. Look for raccoons along streams and lakes, including those in Kawuneeche Valley, Hollowell Park, and Moraine Park.

ABERT'S SQUIRREL

Sciurus aberti

Squirrel family (Sciuridae)

Quick ID: large squirrel with ear tufts, all black or gray with white belly, long fluffy tail

Length: 18–23"   Weight: 1.8–2 lb

The fascinating Abert's squirrel was named to honor Colonel John James Abert, a topographical engineer responsible for mapping the west in the mid-1800s. The common name, tassel-eared squirrel, aptly describes its long ears adorned with conspicuous inch-long stiff hairs. Abert's squirrel's love of false truffles helps the forest habitat to flourish. Fungal spores in the squirrel's waste products develop into the underground mushrooms that aid in the nutrient uptake of ponderosa pines. Remaining active all year, the squirrel's diet also includes pine seeds and the inner bark of succulent Ponderosa pine twigs, which can be consumed at the hearty rate of up to forty-five twigs per day. Look for Abert's squirrels in Ponderosa pine forests near Aspenglen Campground and Endovalley Picnic Area.

GOLDEN-MANTLED GROUND SQUIRREL

Spermophilus lateralis

Squirrel family (Sciuridae)

Quick ID: golden-reddish, whitish belly, no stripes on head, white ring around eye

Length: 9.5–11.5"   Weight: 6–12 oz

With quick movements and bold stripes on its back, the golden-mantled ground squirrel appears to be an overgrown chipmunk. The key to identifying this chipmunk look-alike is the lack of stripes on the head and a white ring around the eye. Found throughout the park, these true squirrels are nearly omnivorous, as they eat a wide variety of foods including fungi, plants, fruits, seeds, insects, eggs, nestling birds, small mammals, and carrion. Unfortunately, they have also become accustomed to visitors, especially in picnic areas in the park. Please do not feed these brazen beggars.

LEAST CHIPMUNK

Tamias minimum

Squirrel family (Sciuridae)

Quick ID: black and white stripes on back and face

Length: 9–10" Weight: 2.3–3.8 oz

The least chipmunk is aptly named, as it is the smallest member of the squirrel family. The other common chipmunk in the park, the Uinta chipmunk, *(Neotamias umbrinus)*, is very similar but a bit larger, with duller coloration and grayish hindquarters. Chipmunks can be distinguished from the larger golden-mantled ground squirrels by the stripes on the face. According to an American Indians legend, the chipmunk teased a bear causing him to become angry and lash out at the chipmunk. The chipmunk got away but not without permanent claw marks on its face and back as a reminder not to make fun of others.

RED SQUIRREL

Tamiasciurus hudsonicus

Squirrel family (Sciuridae)

Quick ID: no stripes, gray to brown or slightly reddish, white belly, white ring around eye

Length: 11–14"   Weight: 6–11 oz

Loud, fearless chatters from treetops may attract the attention of visitors to Rocky Mountain National Park. Proclaiming territorial ownership, the small red squirrel does not warrant alarm—unless you are another squirrel. Commonly called pine squirrels or chickarees, these vocal forest inhabitants are larger than chipmunks and just as gregarious. Males and females are similar in appearance with gray to reddish-brown coats with white bellies. These industrious squirrels busily spend the day gathering conifer cones, seeds, and berries to store for the long winter. They even gather mushrooms to dry as a special winter treat. Look for red squirrels throughout the park's coniferous forests.

WYOMING GROUND SQUIRREL

Spermophilus elegans
Squirrel family (Sciuridae)
Quick ID: drab, buffy-gray squirrel
Length: 10–12" Weight: 9–14 oz

While watching for predators or feeding, Wyoming ground squirrels are in constant motion. Living in underground colonies of several individuals, this species is often mistaken for the larger prairie dog, which is not found in the park.

YELLOW-BELLIED MARMOT

Marmota flaviventris

Squirrel family (Sciuridae)

Quick ID: grizzled brownish-yellow on back, yellowish on belly

Length: 18.5"–2.3' Weight: 4.5–11 lb

The yellow-bellied marmot remains in hibernation later than its famous cousin from the east, the groundhog. Rather than rousing on February 2, the yellow-bellied marmot remains in a state of hibernation until April or May. Look for marmots sunning themselves on rocky areas or surveying the land in high-country meadows. Males may mate with a single female or have harems of up to four females. Marmots reside in burrows protected by large boulders. With a high-pitched whistling shriek, they warn other marmots of predators, such as hawks or other possible dangers. They can be easily spotted along Trail Ridge Road especially at Rock Cut and Lava Cliffs.

BLACK BEAR

Ursus americanus

Bear family (Ursidae)

Quick ID: large, usually black to brownish, light brown snout, round ears, flat-footed walk

Length: 4–6.5' Weight: 86–900 lb

The black bear is the only bear species found in Rocky Mountain National Park, as grizzly bears have not been seen in the park since the early 1900s. They are usually black or dark brown and may have a white patch on the chest. Mainly vegetarians, bears are omnivores and will eat a wide variety of foods including grasses, insects, fruits, acorns, and small mammals. Proper food and garbage storage is important when camping to prevent bear incidents. Fewer than fifty black bears are thought to inhabit Rocky Mountain National Park. Infrequently seen in the park, look for bears along Old Fall River Road.

BIG BROWN BAT

Eptesicus fuscus

Vesper bat family (Vespertilionidae)

Quick ID: brown fur, black face, ears, and wing membranes; wingspan 11-13 inches

Length: 4 – 5" Weight: .33–.81 oz

Nimble acrobats wheeling effortlessly through the night skies, bats use echolocation to find their insect prey. Long maligned as omens of bad luck, bats are important members of the ecosystem, as their voracious appetites for mosquitoes and other flying insects help keep populations of these pests in check. In addition to *Eptesicus fuscus*, seven other species of bats have been found in the park.

GOLDEN EAGLE

Aquila chrysaetos

Diurnal raptor family (Accipitridae)

Quick ID: very large, dark-brown raptor; golden head; long wings

Length: 30" Weight: 10 lb Wingspan: 79"

Visitors to Rocky Mountain National Park have the opportunity to view one of the largest birds of prey, the golden eagle. Majestically soaring over meadows, they often hold their wings in a dihedral or shallow V similar to the flight of the turkey vulture. Along with the less commonly seen bald eagle, "goldens" play an important role in maintaining populations of rodents and other small mammals. Golden eagles take three years to reach adult plumage. Juvenal golden eagles often have a white patch near the end of their wings as well as a white band on the tail. Look for eagles near Lumpy Ridge, Horseshoe Park, and Moraine Park.

NORTHERN GOSHAWK

Accipiter gentilis

Accipiter family (Accipitridae)

Quick ID: slate gray above, gray barring below, white eyebrow (supercilium)

Length: 21" Weight: 2.1 lb Wingspan: 41"

A powerful bird of prey, the northern goshawk has distinctive black-and-white facial markings on its resolute head. The relatively broad wings slice through the air with deep strokes as this agile hunter flies with bullet speed and accuracy through wooded areas. Goshawks prey on grouse and similar birds and small mammals such as ground squirrels and snowshoe hares. Juvenile goshawks are brown with brown streaking. The name *goshawk* comes from the Old English meaning "goose hawk." You may get a glimpse of this elusive and special bird in wooded areas and along forest edges in Moraine Park.

RED-TAILED HAWK

Buteo jamaicensis

Hawk family (Accipitridae)

Quick ID: large hawk with broad, rounded wings; reddish tail; streaked bellyband

Length: 19" Weight: 2.4 lb Wingspan: 49"

One of the most commonly seen raptors in the park, this important predator of small mammals is often spotted with mobs of harrassing ravens, crows, and jays as it circles overhead. Soaring on broad, rounded wings, the adult's upper red tail feathers can sometimes be seen when the hawk banks gracefully in the breeze. Look for these hawks throughout the park, but especially near meadows where they can be seen hunting in open areas.

HORNED LARK

Eremophila alpestris

Lark family (Alaudidae)

Quick ID: black mask on yellow face, pale brownish upperparts, pale belly, dark breast band
Length: 7.25" Weight: 1.1 oz Wingspan: 12"

The horned lark, dubbed "lark of the mountains" by Carl Linnaeus, is often spotted along Trail Ridge Road. In flight, the birds sing a high-pitched tinkling song. Males have curious tufts of feathers on their heads that can be lowered or raised like two horns. Common in alpine tundra, horned larks can be seen walking or running on the ground foraging for seeds and insects. Ground nesters, they weave a basket of grass and other plant materials in which the female broods three to four young. In summer, look for these birds on the tundra along Trail Ridge Road at Forest Canyon Overlook, Lava Cliffs, and Alpine Visitor Center.

BARROW'S GOLDENEYE

Bucephala islandica

Duck, geese, swan family (Anatidae)

Quick ID: medium size, black and white, purplish head, white crescent at base of bill

Length: 18" Weight: 2.1 lb Wingspan: 28"

Sometimes seen on Shadow Mountain Lake, Barrow's goldeneye, was named to honor Sir John Barrow (1764–1848), an English statesman. Barrow's goldeneye and the similar common goldeneye are found on open water in winter as well as spring and fall. Barrow's goldeneye has a white crescent patch on its face in contrast to the white spot of the common goldeneye.

CANADA GOOSE

Branta canadensis

Duck, geese, swan family (Anatidae)

Quick ID: long black neck, white cheeks (chinstrap), brown back, streaked tan breast

Length: 45" Weight: 9.8 lb Wingspan: 60"

In recent years the Canada goose has increased its breeding range south from Canada and the northland and is now the familiar goose of parks and golf courses. They have become resident on large lakes in and around the park such as Shadow Mountain Lake and Lake Estes. Populations are augmented by different subspecies in the winter. Occasionally the smaller cackling geese are seen. Typical of all Canada geese is the white cheek patch, or "chinstrap," that extends below the chin.

COMMON GOLDENEYE

Bucephala clangula

Duck, geese, swan family (Anatidae)

Quick ID: male—black and white, green head, rounded spot at base of bill; female—grayish brown, brown head, mainly dark bill

Length: 18.5" Weight: 1.9 lb Wingspan: 26"

Goldeneyes are small diving ducks that can be found on park lakes. Common goldeneyes in the park outnumber their relative, the Barrow's goldeneye. Males are white with a black head and back. The round spot on their face distinguishes them from Barrow's goldeneyes, whose white face spot is crescent shaped. Female common goldeneyes have a brown head and gray body. Goldeneyes, of course, have eyes that are golden yellow.

COMMON MERGANSER

Mergus merganser

Duck, geese, swan family (Anatidae)

Quick ID: male—greenish head, black back, white body, tapered orange-red bill; female—chestnut head and throat, gray breast, white chin patch

Length: 25" Weight: 3.4 lb Wingspan: 34"

Mergansers are characterized by a long, narrow bill with serrations that help them grasp slippery fish. Common merganser males have a dark head and white body, while females have a rusty brown head and gray body. Both have a slender orange bill. Look for common mergansers on low-elevation park lakes.

MALLARD

Anas platyrhynchos

Duck, geese, swan family (Anatidae)

Quick ID: male—green head, chestnut breast, white neck ring, yellow bill; female—brown, course markings, orange bill with dark splotch in center

Length: 23" Weight: 2.4 lb Wingspan: 35"

The mallard has adapted to human interferences more than any other waterfowl species and, as a result, is now the most familiar species of duck. The male mallard has a yellow bill on a dark green head bordered below by a thin white neck ring. Its brown chest and pale body end with a characteristic curly tail. The female is dull brown with an orange bill. Found in many wetland habitats in the park, mallard ducklings can be seen each spring dabbling in the shallow water at the Sprague Lake picnic area.

RING-NECKED DUCK

Aythya collaris

Duck, geese, swan family (Anatidae)

Quick ID: mediums-size duck, peaked head, bluish bill with white markings; male—black upperparts and gray sides; female—brown back and tan sides

Length: 17"   Weight: 1.5 lb   Wingspan: 25"

Along with mallards, ring-necked ducks can be found enjoying the park's lakes and ponds during the summer. Freshwater diving ducks, they feed on underwater vegetation, aquatic insects, and small fish. The faint brownish collar on the black neck of the male is very difficult to detect in the field, even though the name ring-necked duck would lead one to believe otherwise. The female has a brown back with tan sides, light brown cheeks and a faint white eye ring. Check Sheep Lakes, Lily Lake, and Sprague Lake for these and several other duck and geese species.

BLACK-HEADED GROSBEAK

Pheucticus melanocephalus

Cardinal family (Cardinalidae)

Quick ID: male—black, white, and orange underparts; female—streaky brown

Length: 8.25" Weight: 1.6 oz Wingspan: 12.5"

The brightly colored male black-headed grosbeak is an eye-catching bird of the lower elevations in the park. The inconspicuous female is streaky brown with white markings and pale orange underparts. Grosbeaks possess large heavy bills suitable for crushing seeds, but their diet also includes berries and insects. These birds migrate south for the winter.

WESTERN TANAGER

Piranga ludoviciana

Cardinal family (Cardinalidae)

Quick ID: red-orange head and neck, yellow body, black wings and back

Length: 7.25" Weight: 0.98 oz Wingspan: 11.5"

Few birds can match the striking coloration of the western tanager. With a bright red-orange head and neck, yellow body, and black back and wings, the male is unmistakable. The female is dull yellow with a gray-brown back and yellow wing bars. The bright red plumage of the male is a result of the red pigment rhodoxanthin, which comes presumably from its diet of insects that in turn acquire the pigment from plants. Previously placed in the Tanager family, western tanagers have recently been moved to the Cardinal family. Look for these lovely birds in Endovalley, Upper Beaver Meadows, and the Sprague Lake areas.

TURKEY VULTURE

Cathartes aura

New world vulture family (Cathartidae)

Quick ID: black, silvery flight feathers, bare red head, flight with wings in dihedral

Length: 26" Weight: 4 lb Wingspan: 67"

In April, turkey vultures arrive with the warm spring breezes, soaring with wings held in a shallow V called a dihedral. The two-toned underwing coloration is especially evident as they slowly rock back and forth, rarely flapping, while they search for carrion using their keen sense of smell. Look for these important environmental recyclers at lower elevations in the park.

AMERICAN DIPPER

Cinclus mexicanus

Dipper family (Cinclidae)

Quick ID: gray, stocky body, long legs, short tail

Length: 7.5" Weight: 2 oz Wingspan: 11"

Ouzel Lake and Ouzel Falls in the park share the common name for a very unusual bird. Part fish, part duck, part songbird may best describe this small, chunky gray bird known as the American dipper. Commonly known as water ouzel (pronounced oo-zuhl), this small songbird is always found near cold, fast-moving water. "Ouzel" was a widespread name used for a blackbird in Europe. Hopping from rock to rock, bobbing up and down, the bird hunts for insects by walking underwater along the stream bottom or swimming with its strong wings. Watch for dippers along streams and rivers in the park, especially Roaring River at Alluvial Fan and along North St. Vrain Creek to Ouzel Falls in Wild Basin.

BLACK-BILLED MAGPIE

Pica hudsonia

Crow family (Corvidae)

Quick ID: black and white, long tail, swaggering walk

Length: 19" Weight: 6 oz Wingspan: 25"

The black-billed magpie is well recognized across the western states, but this large crow-sizebird is often a novelty for visitors from the East. The conspicuously long, iridescent tail makes up half the total length of the bird. In flight, the ends of the flight feathers (primaries) have distinctive large white patches. Magpies have a symbiotic relationship with large ungulates and may sometimes be seen picking ticks and other insects from the backs of deer, elk, or moose. Black-billed magpies are year round residents of Rocky Mountain National Park and can be predictably found around the parking areas of Beaver Valley Visitor Center, Moraine Park Visitor Center, and many picnic areas throughout the park.

CLARK'S NUTCRACKER

Nucifraga columbiana

Crow family (Corvidae)

Quick ID: pale gray, black wings with white, pointed black bill, black tail with white outer tail feathers

Length: 12" Weight: 4.6 oz Wingspan: 24"

Its greater size, large black wings with white patch, and long pointed bill help to distinguish Clark's nutcracker from the gray jay. Named for William Clark of the famed Lewis and Clark Expedition, the bird uses its long, sharp bill to open pinecones to feed on the nutritious seeds. It also has a special pouch under its tongue in which it can hold many seeds. A master at storing food reserves for the winter, the bird hides seeds in hundreds to thousands of caches for later use. Surplus seeds often germinate and add new growth to the forest. Look for Clark's nutcrackers at Rainbow Curve, the Lake Irene picnic area, and Moraine Park.

COMMON RAVEN

Corvus corax

Crow family (Corvidae)

Quick ID: large, solid black, long narrow wings, wedge-shaped tail, heavy bill

Length: 24" Weight: 2.6 lb Wingspan: 53"

The raucous call of the common raven is often heard before visitors to the park spy the jet black aerial acrobats free floating through the mountain air. To the delight of bird watchers, ravens will fly upside down and even do loop-de-loops in midair. Along with their smaller cousins, the American crow, ravens often hassle birds of prey when they intrude on their home territory. Even though both birds are totally black, ravens are much larger than crows and have a larger bill and wedge-shaped tail.

GRAY JAY

Perisoreus canadensis

Crow family (Corvidae)

Quick ID: pale gray, short black bill, whitish head with darker gray nape

Length: 11.5" Weight: 2.5 oz Wingspan: 18"

Certainly one of the more observable birds of the park, the gray jay is a member of a trio of avian thieves known as "camp robbers." Along with Clark's nutcracker and Steller's jay, the trio has gained a reputation for skillfully snitching food from unattended picnic tables or camps. Please do not encourage this behavior as it is not only illegal to feed any animals in the park but it is also not healthy for the animals. Gray jays produce unusually sticky saliva, which they use to glue small food items to tree branches. These numerous caches are important for survival in winter. Gray jays, which look something like large chicadees, can often be spotted at the Lake Irene picnic area and Bear Lake.

STELLER'S JAY

Cyanocitta stelleri

Crow family (Corvidae)

Quick ID: azure-blue body, wings, tail; blackish head, breast, back; long crest on head

Length: 11.5" Weight: 3.7 oz Wingspan: 19"

Nothing escapes the vigilant eyes of the Steller's jay, who serves as the daily newscaster of the avian world, loudly announcing the appearance of intruders. Found in wooded areas throughout the park, flocks of Steller's jays often mob predators such as hawks in an attempt to annoy them away from their territory. Georg Steller, a German naturalist, was the first European to describe several North American plants and animals, including the jay that now bears his name. Commonly seen at Many Parks Curve and Hidden Valley, Steller's jays can also be spotted throughout the park.

CHIPPING SPARROW

Spizella passerina

Sparrow Family (Emberizidae)

Quick ID: rufous crown, white eyebrow, black eye stripe, gray breast, gray rump

Length: 5.5" Weight: 0.42 oz Wingspan: 8.5"

Chipping sparrows are frequently seen along meadow edges in Moraine Park, Endovalley and many other areas of the park. They often run on the ground chasing insects or hopping up to feed on grass seeds. The bright rufous cap, black stripe through the eye, and white line over the eye help to identify this petite sparrow. Young chipping sparrows have less distinct, striped rufous caps and are paler overall.

DARK-EYED JUNCO

Junco hyemalis

Sparrow family (Emberizidae)

Quick ID: gray above, white belly, variable pinkish sides, pink bill

Length: 6.25" Weight: 0.67 oz Wingspan: 9.25"

Dark-eyed juncos are one of the most variable species, with at least six different populations across the country. In Rocky Mountain National Park, you can see five of the subspecies of dark-eyed juncos, including gray-headed, Oregon, pink-sided, slate-colored, and white-winged. According to results from the National Audubon Society's Christmas Bird Count the dark-eyed and Oregon subspecies are the most common in the park, followed by slate-colored and white-winged. The gray-headed subspecies is a common summer resident in the park. Found throughout the park, look for juncos at Rainbow Curve, Hidden Valley, and Sheep Lakes.

LINCOLN'S SPARROW

Melospiza lincolnii

Sparrow family (Emberizidae)

Quick ID: medium-small sparrow, streaked brownish upper parts, buffy breast with fine black streaks, white belly, gray facial features

Length: 5.75" Weight: 0.6 oz Wingspan: 7.5"

Lincoln's sparrow shares its name with a famous US president but was actually named by John James Audubon to honor his friend Thomas Lincoln of Maine. Singing a rich musical trill, the birds can be seen skulking through the dense sedges, grasses, and wetland willows habitats. Somewhat similar in appearance to the song sparrow, Lincoln's sparrow is slightly smaller, with black streaks that are finer than the thick streaks of the song sparrow. Lincoln's sparrows glean willow branches for insects, including caterpillars, moths, beetles, and ants. Check in the fenced exclosure across from the Alluvial Fan picnic area for these secretive birds, but please stay on the trail to avoid disturbing them.

WHITE-CROWNED SPARROW

Zonotrichia leucophrys

Sparrow family (Emberizidae)

Quick ID: bold black and white stripes on cap, unstreaked grayish breast, brown-streaked back, pinkish-orange to yellowish bill

Length: 7" Weight: 1 oz Wingspan: 9.5"

A common sparrow of North America, the white-crowned sparrow is easily recognized by the clean white and black stripes on its cap. In the park, these sparrows often breed in willow thickets and can sometimes be found near timberline spruce-fir forests. Look for this sparrow in most areas of the park, including along Tonahutu Creek Trail.

PRAIRIE FALCON

Falco mexicanus

Falcon family (Falconidae)

Quick ID: pale brown above, pale flight feathers with black feathers in axillary (armpit) region

Length: 16" Weight: 1.6 lb Wingspan: 40"

Often spotted soaring over the tundra, the prairie falcons and their relative the peregrine falcon can be seen in the Lumpy Ridge and Cow Creek areas of the park along the cliffs. The larger peregrine falcon has distinct facial markings, longer, more pointed wings, and does not have the dark markings under the "armpit." In contrast to the dramatic plunge hunting of the peregrine falcon, the prairie falcon hunts small mammals and birds with shallow swoops low to the ground. Some trails and areas of the park are closed during nesting season to protect these and other raptors.

BROWN-CAPPED ROSY-FINCH

Leucosticte australis

Finch family (Fringillidae)

Quick ID: medium-size finch, brown head and back, black forehead, rosy-pink belly

Length: 6.25" Weight: 0.91 oz Wingspan: 13"

While the majority of visitors to Rocky Mountain National Park look forward to spotting elk, moose, and bighorn sheep, some nature lovers come here with the hope of catching a glimpse of a small brown finch. A special inhabitant of the alpine tundra of the central Rocky Mountains, the brown-capped rosy-finch is only found in its highest peaks. With a recent decline in numbers, the park is an important bird area that protects necessary habitat for this small tundra-breeding bird. During winter these finches move to lower elevations, but in summer visitors can see them foraging along the edges of snowfields at Lava Cliffs, Rock Cut, and Alpine Visitors Center.

CASSIN'S FINCH

Carpodacus cassinii

Finch family (Fringillidae)

Quick ID: male—rosy red on head and chest; female—striped brown

Length: 6.25" Weight: 0.91 oz Wingspan: 11.5"

Cassin's finches nest in forests throughout the park. Similar in appearance to house finches, the Cassin's finch lacks streaks on the breast, and it has heavier streaking on the face. Other finches sporadically seen in the park in winter include red and white crossbills, pine and evening grosbeaks, and common redpolls.

RED CROSSBILL

Loxia curvirostra

Finch family (Fringillidae)

Quick ID: bill with crossed tips; male—reddish with blackish wings; female—greenish yellow

Length: 6.25" Weight: 1.3 oz Wingspan: 11"

The distinctly crossed, deformed-looking bill of the red crossbill makes this bird uniquely adapted to open the cones of conifers to pluck out the seed. There are several morphs of red crossbills, each specialized to open particular cones. The red crossbill often seen in the park is called the Ponderosa red (type 2), which is especially adapted to extract seeds from ponderosa pine cones. Famous as drifters, these birds move about constantly searching for ripe seed cones in coniferous forests.

PINE SISKIN

Carduelis pinus

Finch family (Fringillidae)

Quick ID: streaky brown overall, yellow wing bar, thin, pointed bill

Length: 5" Weight: 0.53 oz Wingspan: 9"

Unlike most birds in the finch family, the bill of the pine siskin is very thin and ideally shaped for plucking thistle seeds from flower heads. Very similar in appearance to goldfinches, pine siskins have brown streaks overall and strong yellow wingbars. The bill is very pointed in contrast to the thicker bill of the American or lesser goldfinch that are rarely seen in the park. Pine siskins feed in small flocks relishing plentiful seeds and insects found throughout the park especially in coniferous forests.

TREE SWALLOW

Tachycineta bicolor

Swallow family (Hirundinidae)

Quick ID: stocky swallow, white underneath, blue-green on top, white below eye

Length: 5.75" Weight: 0.7 oz Wingspan: 14.5"

Experts at catching insects in midair, swallows are built for speed and agility and have been clocked flying at over 18 miles per hour. Swallows nest in cavities and are particularly fond of aspen groves which are abundant in the park. Tree swallows use the feathers from other birds to line their nests for warmth. Duck feathers are highly prized for lining nests, and swallows put on animated aerial displays as they swoop down over open water to scoop up these trophies. Look for tree swallows flying in groups over lakes and streams in the park, including Lily Lake and Fan Lake.

VIOLET-GREEN SWALLOW

Tachycineta thalassina

Swallow family (Hirundinidae)

Quick ID: small swallow, short tail, long wings, white rump, green back, white above eye

Length: 5.25" Weight: 0.49 oz Wingspan: 13.5"

Feeding on the wing, these tiny aerial bullets sail through the air in search of flying insects that inhabit the park. Often seen in small flocks, violet-green swallows look like stiff-winged paper airplanes as they soar over marshes and wetlands hardly bothering to flap their pointed wings. The shape of their wings help distinguish these swallows from tree swallows, which have a similar white belly but more rounded wings. Black swifts also look like the violet-green swallows, but are darker, less common, and nest behind waterfalls in the park. Look for violet-green swallows flying in groups over Lily Lake, Fan Lake, and Copeland Lake.

BREWER'S BLACKBIRD

Euphagus cyanocephalus

Blackbird family (Icteridae)

Quick ID: male—dark, glossy, purplish green; female—gray brown

Length: 9" Weight: 2.2 oz Wingspan: 15.5"

A common bird of campgrounds, open fields, and parking lots, Brewer's blackbird is an understated element of the avifauna (bird life) of the park. The dark plumage of male "Brewer's" reflects bright sheens of purple and green. Females are dull brown with grayish overtones, a coloring important for camouflage from predators when nesting. Brewer's blackbirds respond rapidly to insect outbreaks capturing as many as five large insects per minute. As well as weed seeds and other plant material, their insect diet includes cutworms, weevils, grasshoppers, termites, and tent caterpillars. In winter, they eat plant material. In 1829, John James Audubon named this bird after Thomas Mayo Brewer, an ornithologist friend from Boston.

RED-WINGED BLACKBIRD

Agelaius phoeniceus

Blackbird family (Icteridae)

Quick ID: male—shiny black, red with yellow border on shoulder; female—streaky brown
Length: 8.75" Weight: 1.8 oz Wingspan: 13"

Even though this may be the most numerous bird in North America, many people do not recognize this bird and wonder what the black bird with red patches on the shoulder could be. Once recognized, the red-winged blackbird is easy to identify, as the red-and-yellow shoulder patches are unmistakable. To proclaim their territory, males repeatedly call a loud *ko-ka-ree* call while displaying their wings and red shoulder patches. Totally different in plumage than the male, females resemble a large sparrow clothed in dull brown streaks. Quite busy, one male red-winged blackbird may defend up to fifteen nesting females on its territory in wetlands.

NORTHERN SHRIKE

Lanius excubitor

Shrike family (Laniidae)

Quick ID: gray back, black face mask, wings black with white patch, white throat and chest

Length: 10" Weight: 2.3 oz Wingspan: 14.5"

A medium-size songbird, the northern shrike is the ultimate predator. Fast, powerful, and fully equipped to strike with amazing accuracy, the shrike zeros in on its prey with focused intent. Preying on insects, small mammals, and other birds, the northern shrike monitors its surroundings from an exposed perch, such as a tree branch, post, or wire. Its large, hooked bill helps to subdue its prey, which it often impales on thorns or barbed wire. This method of storing excess food for leaner times has earned this natural predator the nickname "butcher bird."

AMERICAN PIPIT

Anthus rubescens

Pipit family (Motacillidae)

Quick ID: slender, sparrow-size, brown, bobs tail when walking

Length: 6.5"   Weight: 0.74 oz   Wingspan: 10.5"

One of the few songbirds that nest on the alpine tundra, the American pipit braves extreme conditions to take advantage of the abundance of summer insect broods. This sparrow-size bird has noticeable white on the outer edges of its tail but its faintly streaked grayish-brown feathers blend in well with the grasses of the tundra landscape. Like a drum major leading the parade, this slender bird marches about upright while bobbing its tail up and down. Look for American pipits along the roadsides as you drive on Trail Ridge Road including pullovers at Rock Cut, Lava Cliffs, and Medicine Bow Curve.

BLACK-CAPPED CHICKADEE

Poecile atricapillus

Chickadee and titmice family (Paridae)

Quick ID: black cap, white cheeks, black chin, gray wings with white edging

Length: 5.25" Weight: 0.39 oz Wingspan: 8"

A familiar and favorite bird, the black-capped chickadee is a delight to watch in action. Flitting from branch to branch, these busy birds glean insects, spiders, and caterpillars, stopping only long enough to wipe their tiny bills on a branch. Their characteristic, frequent *chika-dee-dee* call is easily identified. Full of feisty bold attitude, chickadees are very territorial and will often mob predators giving a sharp "zeet" alarm call. Found year-round in the park, black-capped chickadees are regularly counted during the National Audubon Society's Christmas Bird Count, which shows they are outnumbered by the more numerous mountain chickadees. Listen and look for these birds along Cub Lake Trail and the Endovalley picnic area.

MOUNTAIN CHICKADEE

Poecile gambeli

Chickadee and titmice family (Paridae)

Quick ID: white eyebrow, black line through eye, gray wings, black cap, white cheeks, black chin

Length: 5.25" Weight: 0.39 oz Wingspan: 8.5"

This small, scrappy resident of Rocky Mountain National Park is a familiar bird to most visitors and is easily seen throughout the park. The mountain chickadee has a prominent white feathered eyebrow that helps to distinguish it from its relative the black-capped chickadee. Chickadees eat large numbers of insects, including the bark beetles and needle miners that infect trees. They sometimes cling acrobatically to twigs or conifer cones as they forage for insects. In autumn, they busily cache conifer seeds for the winter ahead. Found throughout the park in forested areas, they're easily spotted in campgrounds, including Moraine Park, Aspenglen, Endovalley, and Glacier Basin.

WILSON'S WARBLER

Wilsonia pusilla

Wood-warbler family (Parulidae)

Quick ID: small warbler, lemon yellow, dark eye; male—black cap; female—duller cap

Length: 4.75" Weight: 0.27 oz Wingspan: 7"

Wilson's warbler is an inquisitive small bird common in willow thickets and other scrubby wetland areas of the park. A neotropical migrant, Wilson's warbler spends the colder months in Mexico and Central America, then returns to North America to breed. Wilson's warblers glean insects as they hop from branch to branch, all the while waving their tail. This and several other bird species were named to honor a Scottish naturalist named Alexander Wilson, whose work in the early 1800s earned him the honor of being regarded as one of America's greatest ornithologists. Look for these small yellow gems in the wetlands near Endovalley Picnic Area, Tonahutu Trail, Sprague Lake Trail, and Moraine Park.

YELLOW-RUMPED WARBLER

Dendroica coronata

Wood-warbler family (Parulidae)

Quick ID: large warbler; gray and black; bright-yellow throat, rump, and sides

Length: 5.5" Weight: 0.43 oz Wingspan: 9.25"

A widespread warbler, the yellow-rumped warbler has two distinct subspecies. The somewhat duller "myrtle" warbler inhabits eastern North America while the brighter "Audubon's" warbler lives in the west. These busy warblers forage among trees and may be seen fluttering in the air to catch flying insects. These small birds play an important role in maintaining insect populations as they thrive on beetles, ants, aphids, grasshoppers, spiders, gnats, and weevils. They also eat spruce budworms, which are major defoliators of firs and spruce. Berries are also eaten in the fall. Look for "yellow-rumps" at forest openings along Old Fall River Road, Bear Lake Trail, and Ouzel Falls Trail.

AMERICAN WHITE PELICAN

Pelecanus erythrorhynchos

Pelican family (Pelecanidae)

Quick ID: very large, white, black outer wing feathers, yellow bill and gular pouch

Length: 62" Weight: 16.4 lb Wingspan: 108"

Soaring majestically over the Rockies, these white hang gliders of nature travel through the skies in straight lines or form V-shaped squadrons. The 9-foot wingspan and 4-foot height of the American white pelican makes it one of the largest birds in North America. Pelicans make use of their large yellow expandable pouch to scoop up fish to carry back to their young. In breeding season, the adults develop a fibrous plate on their bill like a small fin. This bill plate or nuptial tubercle is used for mating displays and eventually falls off after mating season. Pelicans may be seen on Shadow Mountain Lake and even flying over the tundra.

DUSKY GROUSE

Dendragapus obscurus

Upland game bird family (Phasianidae)

Quick ID: stocky, chickenlike, long neck and tail, brown to bluish-gray mottling

Length: 20" Weight: 2.3 lb Wingspan: 26"

Formally known as the blue grouse, the dusky grouse is a master in two disciplines: camouflage and comedy. These quiet chickenlike birds forage along forest edges, but during the spring courting season the low hoots of males sound a bit like air blowing across a bottle. In a comical mating display, the male flaunts red-orange "eyebrow" feathers and he puffs out curious raspberry-colored neck air sacs surrounded by a circle of bright white feathers. Showing little fear of humans, the dusky grouse can sometimes be observed in the Wild Basin area (look around the edges of the parking area), Old Fall River Road, or Fern Lake trailhead.

WHITE-TAILED PTARMIGAN

Lagopus leucurus

Upland game bird family (Phasianidae)

Quick ID: stocky; chickenlike; brownish-gray in summer, white in winter

Length: 12.5"   Weight: 13 oz Wingspan: 22"

In a marvelous design of survival strategy, the feathers of the white-tailed ptarmigan change with the seasons. Totally white in winter, this well-insulated bird is one of the few creatures that can withstand the extreme weather conditions of the tundra year-round. Slowly transitioning in a checkerboard fashion, these masters of camouflage molt into a cloaked outfit of mottled gray-brown feathers. Blending in spectacularly with the tundra surroundings and possessing the ability to remain incredibly motionless, it is quite easy to pass very close to the rock-still bird without noticing it. In summer, try to spot these masters of concealment at Rainbow Curve, Medicine Bow Curve, and on tundra trails near the Alpine Visitor Center.

AMERICAN THREE-TOED WOODPECKER

Picoides tridactylus

Woodpecker family (Picidae)

Quick ID: medium-size, black-and white, white back, golden spot on forehead

Length: 8.75" Weight: 2.3 oz Wingspan: 15"

Most woodpeckers have two toes forward and two toes backward, but the American three-toed woodpecker is missing one of the back toes. An irruptive species that moves into areas that have experienced fire or insect damage, this woodpecker is perhaps one of the few Rocky Mountain inhabitants that has enjoyed the damaging effects of the pine bark beetle on trees in the park. Similar in size and coloration to the hairy woodpecker, the three-toed woodpecker has a yellow spot on its forehead, in contrast to the red spot on the hairy. Look for these uncommon woodpeckers in boreal and montane coniferous forests as they forage by flaking off loose bark in areas such as Milner Pass and Endovalley.

HAIRY WOODPECKER

Picoides villosus

Woodpecker family (Picidae)

Quick ID: white-and-black back; white underparts; male—red on back of head

Length: 9.25" Weight: 2.3 oz Wingspan: 15"

A challenge for beginning birders, the plumage of a hairy woodpecker is very similar to that of a downy woodpecker, except for the black dots in the downy's white outer tail feathers. A hairy woodpecker is about 3 inches longer than a downy woodpecker. The bill of a hairy woodpecker is almost as long as its head in comparison with the much smaller bill of the downy woodpecker. The adult males of both species have a red patch on their head, while the females lack the red patch. The hairy woodpecker is more common in the park than the downy woodpecker and can be found in many wooded areas.

RED-NAPED SAPSUCKER

Sphyrapicus nuchalis

Woodpecker family (Picidae)

Quick ID: medium-size, black-and-white barring, white bar on sides, red throat and forehead, yellow belly

Length: 8.5" Weight: 1.8 oz Wingspan: 16"

With a fire-engine-red forehead and throat, the red-naped sapsucker adds a colorful element to the forests of Rocky Mountain. Sometimes names can be a bit misleading, as is the case with sapsuckers. These birds to not actually suck the sap, but instead they sip it. With their sharp, pointed bills, they drill a series of horizontal holes in trees in which high-energy sap accumulates. Their tongues have specialized hair-like projections that aid in picking up the sticky sap. Other birds, including hummingbirds and warblers, also drink the sugary syrup from these sap wells. Check the Tonahutu Spur Trail near the Kawuneeche Visitor Center for these birds as well as Endovalley area.

WILLIAMSON'S SAPSUCKER

Sphyrapicus thyroideus

Woodpecker family (Picidae)

Quick ID: medium-size, yellow belly; male—mostly black with white markings, red chin patch; female—brown barred, brown head

Length: 9" Weight: 1.8 oz Wingspan: 17"

Bearing the name of Lieutenant Robert Stockton Williamson, a topographical engineer who took part in western surveying expeditions in the mid-1800s, Williamson's sapsucker is unique in the woodpecker world. Most male and female woodpeckers display similar plumages, but males and females of this species are so unlike that they appear to be different species. They so puzzled early naturalists that these birds underwent many name changes, including black-breasted woodpecker, brown-headed woodpecker, round-headed woodpecker, and Williamson's woodpecker. It was not until 1873 that these radically different birds were observed nesting together by Henry W. Henshaw, a naturalist working on an ornithological survey of western birds. Look for these birds along the road just north of Alluvial Fan parking area and around Upper Beaver Meadows.

RUBY-CROWNED KINGLET

Regulus calendula

Kinglet family (Regulidae)

Quick ID: small, olive-green, white eye ring; male—red crown

Length: 4.25"   Weight: 0.23 oz   Wingspan: 7.5"

Ruby-crowned kinglets are tiny hyperactive birds constantly on the move, flicking their wings as they glean insects from tree branches. Male ruby-crowned kinglets have hidden ruby-red head feathers that they display when agitated. These birds breed in spruce-fir forests in the park. In the winter they leave their relatives, golden-crowned kinglets, behind for warmer climates in the south.

SPOTTED SANDPIPER

Actitis macularia

Sandpiper family (Scolopacidae)

Quick ID: brown back, white underparts with black spots, orange bill and feet

Length: 7.5" Weight: 1.4 oz Wingspan: 15"

Spotted sandpipers are shorebirds specially adapted for wading in shallow water. As they forage for insects and water invertebrates, they constantly bob their rear end and tail, teetering up and down. Other commonly seen shorebirds that can be found in the park are killdeer and common snipe. Look for spotted sandpipers along the shores of lakes and streams, including Lily Lake and Sprague Lake.

PYGMY NUTHATCH

Sitta pygmaea

Nuthatch family (Sittidae)

Quick ID: tiny bird, gray body and wings, buffy white belly

Length: 4.25" Weight: 0.37 oz Wingspan: 7.75"

Social birds, pygmy nuthatches often travel in groups, foraging and watching for predators as they call to each other with short high-pitched "squeaky toy" peeps. These tiny birds move up and down tree trunks and branches hunting for insects. Cavity nesters, females lay an average of seven eggs in dead trees, which are called "snags." Older siblings may help the parents feed and care for the hatchlings. To withstand the frigid night temperatures, as many as one hundred pygmy nuthatches may huddle together in a single cavity. Look for these birds throughout the park in forested areas.

GREAT HORNED OWL

Bubo virginianus

Owl family (Strigidae)

Quick ID: very large owl, ear tufts, yellow eyes with grayish facial disks

Length: 22" Weight: 3.1 lb Wingspan: 44"

Masters of the night, great horned owls chant their low hoots through the forests and high meadows of Rocky Mountain National Park. Male great horned owls are smaller than females but have a lower-pitched call. Listen for them calling back and forth just before and after the sun sets behind the mountains. Mainly nocturnal predators, great horned owls subdue their prey with needle-sharp talons. They can take prey weighing up to three times their own weight. Their hooked bills are superbly adept at the job of making bite-size meals. These year-round residents of the park are most easily spotted at dusk, perched on branches overlooking open areas near Alluvial Fan or Moraine Park.

NORTHERN SAW-WHET OWL

Aegolius acadicus

Owl family (Strigidae)

Quick ID: small owl, buffy facial disc, short tail, white spots on brown back and wings

Length: 8" Weight: 2.8 oz Wingspan: 17"

One of the small owls found in the park, the northern saw-whet owl is nocturnal and therefore not often seen by most park visitors. Nevertheless many saw-whet owls inhabit the park's mixed forests. Other small owls found in the park include boreal owl, northern pygmy-owl, and flammulated owl.

BROAD-TAILED HUMMINGBIRD

Selasphorus platycercus

Hummingbird family (Trochilidae)

Quick ID: metallic green crown and back; male—rosy-red throat; female—white throat with greenish-bronze spots, some rufous on broad tail

Length: 4" Weight: 0.13 oz Wingspan: 5.25"

Broad-tailed hummingbirds are the most common members of their family found in the park. These sparkling jewels migrate back to their Rocky Mountain breeding grounds in April and early May to take advantage of the flowering plants and insects. They have special survival techniques when temperatures drop below freezing. On their roost, the tiny birds enter a state of physiologic torpor as their heart rate slows and body temperature drops. This slowed metabolic state allows them to maintain a body temperature of about 54 degrees even when the ambient temperatures fall below freezing. Look for these hummers feeding on tubular flowers in the nature garden at Beaver Valley Visitor Center and the Bowen-Baker trailhead picnic area.

RUFOUS HUMMINGBIRD

Selasphorus rufus

Hummingbird family (Trochilidae)

Quick ID: males—rufous, red gorget; female—back green, rufous sides, tail feathers with rufous

Length: 3.75" Weight: 0.12 oz Wingspan: 4.5"

Rascal of the hummingbird world, the rufous hummingbird aggressively defends its territory by dive-bombing other hummers and even bees that would steal the nectar from its flowers. Aptly named "rufous" for its rusty-orange coloration, the male sports a brilliant red throat patch called a "gorget," while the greener female has a white throat with green specks, often with a spot of red-orange. Look for these feisty hummers from early July through the fall, especially around the Beaver Meadows Visitor Center flower garden.

HOUSE WREN

Troglodytes aedon

Wren family (Troglodytidae)

Quick ID: small, brown, faint barring on wings, thin, decurved bill

Length: 4.75" Weight: 0.39 oz Wingspan: 6"

Most people hear the fizzy, bubbly song of the house wren long before they see it. The rather plain brown coloration of this small bird, about the size of a chickadee, helps to keep it camouflaged from predators. Cavity nesters, they will often set up house in woody, brushy areas inside tree holes. To aid in ridding their nests of parasites such as mites, the house wrens carry spider egg sacs into the nest; when the spiders hatch, they help keep numbers of mites in check.

AMERICAN ROBIN

Turdus migratorius

Thrush family (Turdidae)

Quick ID: Upperparts gray to black, breast and underparts reddish orange

Length: 10" Weight: 2.7 oz Wingspan: 17"

With its merry song of "cheery, cheerily, cheer up," the American robin is one of the most familiar of all birds. It is a member of the thrush family, along with western bluebirds, hermit and Swainson's thrush, and Townsend's solitaire. The American robin is similar in coloration to a European bird historically known as "robin redbreast" and now called "European robin," a bird that belongs to the flycatcher family and is not at all related to our robin.

MOUNTAIN BLUEBIRD
Sialia currucoides
Thrush family (Turdidae)
Quick ID: male—azure blue; female—pale gray with blue-tinged wings and tail
Length: 7.25" Weight: 1 oz Wingspan: 14"

After spending the cold winter months in the south, mountain bluebirds return to Rocky Mountain National Park in spring to breed and raise their brood. Renowned hunters, these small, alert birds often hover above their insect prey in a movement birders call "hawking." They often perch on exposed limbs overlooking open meadows, and when an insect is spotted, they swoop down to grab it with their bills. Cavity nesters, these birds make their homes in dead or dying trees called "snags." Look for these blue jewels at Sheep Lakes Overlook, Moraine Park, and along Tonahutu Trail.

TOWNSEND'S SOLITAIRE

Myadestes townsendi

Thrush family (Turdidae)

Quick ID: plain gray overall, white eye ring, white outer tail feathers, buffy wing patches

Length: 8.5" Weight: 1.2 oz Wingspan: 14.5"

Smaller and slimmer than a robin and a bit bigger than a bluebird, Townsend's solitaire is a plain gray bird with a white ring around the eye. In flight, you may notice white outer tail feathers like those of the junco. A year-round resident of the park, it is often seen singing sweetly from the top of a tree in the high country. In winter, the bird makes a short altitudinal migration to lower elevations. Townsend's solitaire feeds on the blueberrylike fleshy cones of junipers and is often found where these woody plants are located. In 1838, John James Audubon described and named the species to honor John Kirk Townsend, the early western explorer and naturalist who first discovered the species.

CORDILLERAN FLYCATCHER

Empidonax occidentalis

Tyrant flycatcher family (Tyrannidae)

Quick ID: brownish yellow-olive overall, white eye ring, buffy wing bars

Length: 5.5" Weight: 0.39 oz Wingspan: 8"

Along with Dusky, Hammond's, olive-sided and willow flycatchers, the Cordilleran flycatcher is a small yellowish flycatcher that nests in the park. The white teardrop-shaped eye ring helps distinguish the Cordilleran flycatcher from the others. Until 1989, the Cordilleran flycatcher was formerly known as the "western flycatcher." In 1989, ornithologists distinguished this flycatcher from its look-alike, the Pacific-slope flycatcher, which is found in more western states, including California, Oregon, and Washington. Look for Cordilleran and other flycatchers at Lumpy Ridge, Endovalley, and Moraine Park.

WESTERN WOOD-PEWEE

Contopus sordidulus

Tyrant flycatcher family (Tyrannidae)

Quick ID: grayish above, pale below, whitish wingbars, mostly dark bill

Length: 6.25" Weight: 0.45 oz Wingspan: 10.5"

Western wood-pewees can be heard singing a buzzy "peeeer" from open perches throughout the park. A member of the tyrant flycatcher family, these birds eat a variety of flying insects including flies, bees, and moths that they capture in mid-air, often returning to the original perch. Western wood-pewees and other flycatchers, such as Hammond's and Dusky flycatcher, spend their winters in South America.

WARBLING VIREO

Vireo gilvus

Vireo family (Vireonidae)

Quick ID: olive-grayish-brown above, pale gray below, whitish line through eye, no wingbars

Length: 5.5" Weight: 0.4 oz Wingspan: 8.5"

A common songbird in the park, the warbling vireo is heard more often than it is actually seen. The dull feather coloration helps hide it among the tall branches of aspen and other deciduous trees as it hunts for insects. Listen for the buzzy, choppy, high-pitched song that ends with a descending note; it's quite different from the warble of this vireo found in the east. Endovalley and Upper Beaver Meadows are good spots to look and listen for the warbling vireo.

CLUB HORNED GRASSHOPPER

Aeropedellus clavatus

Grasshopper family (Acrididae)

Quick ID: gray to green with various markings

Size: 1⁄10–8⁄10"

One of the highest-ranging species of grasshopper in North America, the club horned grasshopper feeds on grasses and sedges above timberline in the park. In the Rockies, it has been found at altitudes reaching 13,600 feet. The female nymph is shown here. In the plains habitat, populations can become abundant especially after sufficient rains. Males either have long or short wings and fly extensively. The wings of females are short and they are incapable of flying. Females hop away from predators, but males hop away and prance up and down. This grasshopper of the alpine tundra can be seen along Old Fall River Road, Trail Ridge Road, and alpine trails in the park.

SPECKLE-WINGED RANGELAND GRASSHOPPER

Arphia conspersa

Grasshopper family (Acrididae)

Quick ID: brown body, yellow abdomen, red on wings in flight

Size: 1–1⅛"

Grasshoppers such as the speckle-winged rangeland grasshopper form the food staple for many higher vertebrates. Look for these and other grasshoppers in Moraine Park and other grassy meadows.

WRANGLER GRASSHOPPER

Circotettix rabula

Grasshopper family (Acrididae)

Quick ID: yellow hind wings

Size: 1½–1⅔"

Males give off a loud crackling noise in flight. This grasshopper is highly camouflaged against the rocky hillside along Old Fall River Road.

PADDLE-TAILED DARNER

Aeshna palmata

Darner family (Aeshnidae)

Quick ID: brown; male–blue markings; female–green markings

Size: 2¾"

Paddle-tailed darners can be seen around lake edges in the park. The larva are fierce predators in their underwater environment.

WHITE-SPOTTED SAWYER

Monochamus scutellatus

Longhorned beetle family (Cerambycidae)

Quick ID: shiny black with white spots, long black antennae that can match body length

Size: ¾–1"

The white-spotted sawyer is a large beetle with antennae twice as long as its body. Native beetles, they are found in coniferous forests where they gnaw on the bark of small twigs, damaging the tips and causing them to look like rusty red flags among the other green needles. They usually attack only dead or dying trees especially after fire or storm damage, therefore aiding in the recycling of the forest. Noisy eaters, the larvae sound like small handsaws inside the tree, hence the name "sawyer." In the spring, they chew their way back to the surface, then emerge as adults. Even though these insects are capable of biting, they only do so when they feel threatened or trapped.

LEWIS'S RABBITBUSH LEAF BEETLE

Trirhabda lewisii

Leaf beetle family (Chrysomelidae)

Quick ID: striped yellow and dark markings

Size: ¼ – ⅜"

Leaf beetles are often considered agricultural pests but the plant that Lewis's rabbitbush leaf beetle feeds on is often a pest itself. After spending the winter underground, eggs hatch in April and the caterpillarlike glossy larva begin to feed on the tender young foliage of rabbitbush. After tunneling through the roots the larva form pupa in the soil. Continuing the life cycle, yellow-striped adults emerge in summer and continue to feed on the plant eventually laying eggs that will complete the cycle. Look for the beetles wherever rabbitbush is found in the park.

BLACK-LEGGED MOSQUITO

Ochlerotatus sp.
Mosquito family (Culicidae)
Quick ID: black with long legs
Size: ½"

Of the more than 2,500 species of mosquitoes in the world, about 42 species of mosquitoes are found in Colorado. Weighing only 1/23,000 of an ounce, only female mosquitoes bite, as they need the protein found in blood to nourish their eggs. Male mosquitoes feed on nectar from plants. Some people give off more heat and carbon dioxide than others do, which often attracts more insects, and this is how the female mosquito detects her hosts. Mosquito saliva contains anticoagulants that prevent blood from clotting. These chemicals cause the swelling and itching associated with mosquito bites. To avoid mosquito bites and the potential diseases that they can carry, use an insect repellent especially near wetlands or in the evening.

MOUNTAIN PINE BEETLE

Dendroctonus ponderosa

Weevil and snout beetle family (Curculionidae)

Quick ID: small, black

Size: ⅛–⅓"

Even though you may never see this beetle, which is about the size of a grain of rice, you will certainly be able to see its effects. As far as the eye can see, mountainsides are colored with an ominous rust-red shadow indicating dead or dying trees. Advancing like a slow-motion plague, these beetles have moved from the Grand Lake area to the east side of the park. When a tree is attacked, it attempts to defend itself by producing resin or pitch in an attempt to trap the insects. As the beetles tunnel through the trees they carry with them the spores of a bluestain fungus *(Ceratocystis sp.)*. Colonizing the sapwood, the fungus blocks resin production, circumventing the defenses of the tree.

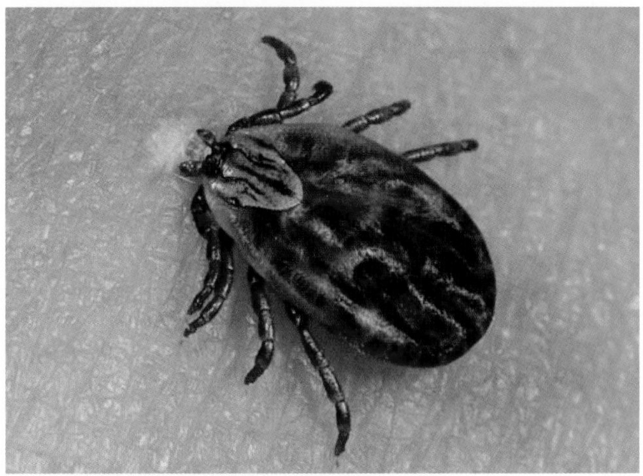

ROCKY MOUNTAIN WOOD TICK

Dermacentor andersoni

Hard tick family (Ixodidae)

Quick ID: rounded brown body

Size: 0.09-0.2"

Not much larger than a big sesame seed, the Rocky Mountain wood tick is a common species of tick in the western United States. Ticks are parasites that require blood from a host to survive. Ticks can carry bacteria and parasites that cause diseases such as Rocky Mountain spotted fever, tularemia and others. Meadows and grassy areas often harbor ticks waiting for a host to pass by. See Safety Notes in the Introduction for more information.

BLACK MEADOWHAWK

Sympetrum danae

Skimmer family (Libellulidae)

Quick ID: Male—almost entirely black with few yellow markings; Female—mostly yellow with black markings

Size: 1.2"

Male and female dragonflies can sometimes be seen joined together either sitting or flying in a mating ritual. Males and females can look quite different in size and coloration. Male black meadowhawks are almost entirely black while females are mostly yellow and may be mistaken as another species of dragonfly. Look for black meadowhawks and other dragonflies along the edge of streams, ponds and wetlands including Lily Lake, Bear Lake and Copeland Lake.

BLISTER BEETLE

Zonitis sp.

Blister beetle family (Meloidae)

Quick ID: yellow

Size: ½–¾"

Similar in coloration to mountain gumweed, *Grindelia subalpina,* this blister beetle is hard for predators to spot. Blister beetles are well named as they secrete a defensive chemical called cantharidin that causes blistering of the skin and membranes. The male beetle secretes the poisonous substance and it is passed to the female during mating. The eggs are then covered with the substance as a defense against predators. Historically, the chemical has been used for medicinal purposes including rheumatism, gout, warts, and even as an aphrodisiac called Spanish fly. The toxic properties are comparable to those of cyanide and strychnine; consequently, ingestion can be fatal. Scientists are currently investigating the use of a derivative of cantharidin in promising cancer treatments.

JUMPING SPIDER

Phidippus sp.

Jumping spider family (Salticidae)

Quick ID: gray, hairy

Size: ⅛–⅝"

Jumping spiders make up over 10 percent of the 35,000 species of spiders in the world. In Colorado, there are about 600 different species of spiders. Jumping spiders are masters of stealth, as they can remain motionless and camouflaged until an unsuspecting prey wanders by. With extremely acute vision, they locate their prey to initiate a surprise attack. Their legs are specialized to utilize internal fluid pressure. Acting like an internal hydraulic system, it literally launches the spider many times its own length in its surprise attacks on insect victims. Spiders are important predators and help to control populations of potentially problematic insects such as flies and ants.

POLICE CAR MOTH/GREEN LATTICE

Gnophaela vermiculata
Tiger moth family
(Arctiidae)
Quick ID: black-and-white pattern
Wingspan: 2"
Flight Season: July–August

While most moths are active at night, the police car moth, sometimes called green lattice, is a day-flying tiger moth. Shown here feeding on yarrow, the striking black-and-white pattern on the wings generated the common name police car moth. The caterpillars feed on chiming bells or bluebells *(Mertensia sp)* which can be found in moist areas of the park including along Green Mountain Trail or Sprague Lake.

TAXILES SKIPPER

Poanes taxiles
Skipper family
(Hesperiidae)
Quick ID: burnt orange, yellow patches on hind wings
Wingspan: 1¼–1⅜"
Flight Season: June–August

Skippers make up about one third of all the butterfly species in North America. Even for expert lepidopterists, they are challenging to identify because their differences are often subtle. Many skippers such as the taxiles skipper have orange and brown wings with yellowish markings. Formerly called golden skipper, the taxiles skipper is common in the park, especially in flower-filled meadows.

HOARY ELFIN
Callophrys polios
Gossamer-wing family (Lycaenidae)
Quick ID: frosted gray to dark brown
Wingspan: 1–1⅛"
Flight Season: April–June

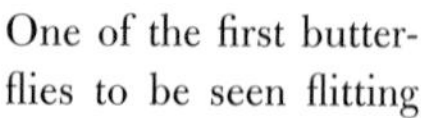

One of the first butterflies to be seen flitting on warm spring breezes is the hoary elfin. The food plant of the caterpillars is kinnikinnick or bearberry, and these small gray-frosted butterflies can often be seen on or near these plants. Look for them in Moraine Park and around Lily Lake.

ROCKY MOUNTAIN AZURE
Celastrina echo sidara
Gossamer-wing family (Lycaenidae)
Quick ID: blue upper wings, underwings gray with brown markings
Wingspan: ⅞–1⅜"
Flight Season: May–June

The Rocky Mountain azure is a subspecies of a wide-ranging complex of small butterflies called spring azures. One of the first butterflies to emerge in the spring, azures typically perch with their wings closed so the blue is usually only seen in flight. They often gather around mud puddles in "puddle parties" to sip moisture and minerals from the damp soil. Look for this small butterfly on the eastern side of the park along the Cow Creek Trail and at Moraine Park Visitor Center.

COMMON ALPINE
Erebia epipsodea
Brushfoot family
(Nymphalidae)
Quick ID: dark brown, orange patches, medium size
Wingspan: 1¾–2"
Flight Season: June–August

The front two feet of the butterflies in the brushfoot family, Nymphalidae, are modified into "windshield wipers" used to wipe pollen off their eyes. A widespread boreal species, the highly adaptable common alpine butterfly ranges from Alaska to New Mexico. The common alpine has orange encircled spots that look like eyes, appropriately called "eyespots," on hind wings.

COMMON RINGLET
Coenonympha tullia
Brushfoot family
(Nymphalidae)
Quick ID: wing underside orange brown, one eyespot on forewing
Wingspan: 1⅓–1½"
Flight Season: May–July

The common ringlet is widespread but often overlooked, as its small size and soft colors make it inconspicuous. It is also known as ochre ringlet due to the pale orange-brown coloration of the upper wings. These butterflies are commonly spotted along roadways, picnic areas and campgrounds including Upper Beaver Meadows and Moraine Park.

MELISSA ARCTIC

Oeneis melissa

Brushfoot family

(Nymphalidae)

Quick ID: brownish-black, mottled black and gray

Wingspan: 1⅝–2"

Flight Season: June–August

A master of camouflage, this medium-size butterfly uses its dark mottled coloration to blend invisibly with the lichen-covered rocky terrain of the tundra. Like all butterflies of the tundra, it flies low to the ground seeking nectar from miniscule wildflowers that hug the ground. In July, it can be seen sunning against mottled rocks at Lava Cliffs and Ute Trail on Trail Ridge Road. A similar dark butterfly of the tundra, the Magdalena Alpine, is all black.

MILBERT'S TORTOISESHELL

Aglais milberti

Brushfoot family

(Nymphalidae)

Quick ID: blackish brown with orange band, jagged edges

Wingspan: 1⅝–2"

Flight Season: March–September

A French entomologist, Jean Baptiste Godart, studied the butterflies of North America and in 1826 named this butterfly for a Mr. Milbert. Milbert's tortoiseshells often bask in the sunlight, revealing their bright orange-and-yellow stripe on jagged brown wings. The adults overwinter in hollow logs or other sheltered places and emerge in early spring. The adults feed on sap, animal dung, and also nectar on a variety of flowers. Like some of its relatives, the status of this striking butterfly varies from year to year. Keep an eye out for these colorful butterflies sunning themselves, especially in the afternoon, on trails or along Old Fall River Road.

PURPLISH FRITILLARY

Boloria montinus
Brushfoot family (Nymphalidae)
Quick ID: orange with black markings
Wingspan: 1¼–1¾"
Flight Season: June–August

Rocky Mountain National Park has many medium- to large-size orange-and-black butterflies that are similar in appearance. Purplish fritillaries often sit with their wings spread as they sip nectar on flat-topped flowers. Butterfly researchers, or lepidopterists, are currently studying the taxonomic relationships between this distinctive species of the southern Rockies and other similar fritillaries to determine their proper classification. Purplish fritillaries are found throughout most of boreal Canada and also have a healthy population in the Southern Rockies. The caterpillars (larvae) feed on plants such as willows and bistorts. Look for this butterfly cruising over subalpine and alpine meadows at the Milner Pass area and the Colorado River trailhead.

WEIDEMEYER'S ADMIRAL

Limenitis weidemeyerii
Brushfoot family (Nymphalidae)
Quick ID: black with white band
Wingspan: 2¾–3¾"
Flight Season: May–September

A striking butterfly with an unusual name, Weidemeyer's admiral is easy to identify. It is a large black butterfly with a broad white band on its wings that is often seen flying high in the treetops including along Old Fall River Road. The adults are territorial and will vigorously fly out to chase off other approaching butterflies. Adorned with mottled gray and white coloration, curious humps, and ornate projections, the caterpillar resembles a large bird dropping with horns. The caterpillars feed on the leaves of willows and aspens. This butterfly is named for John William Weidemeyer, an author and entomologist. In 1864, he wrote the *Catalogue of North American Butterflies*, which was an important compilation of species from Panama to Greenland.

PALE SWALLOWTAIL

Papilio eurymedon
Swallowtail family (Papilionidae)
Quick ID: pale creamy-yellow and black; orange and blue markings
Wingspan: 2¾–3½"
Flight Season: May–July

Several yellow swallowtail butterflies can be found in the park, including the pale swallowtail. The pale swallowtail is paler yellow than both the western tiger swallowtail and the two-tailed swallowtail. The black border on the pale swallowtail also stands out. The anise swallowtail is nearly half black and yellow. Look for these and other swallowtails along Fern Lake Trail, Big Meadows, and Cow Creek Trail.

ROCKY MOUNTAIN PARNASSIAN

Parnassius smintheus
Swallowtail family (Papilionidae)
Quick ID: white with black markings, red spots
Wingspan: 1¾–2½"
Flight Season: May–September

Common throughout the park, Rocky Mountain Parnassians can be seen as early as May in the montane region up to the alpine zone beginning in July. Members of the subfamily, Parnassians, these butterflies lack tails and sport zebra-striped black-and-white antenna. The caterpillars feed on stonecrop, so the females may be seen laying eggs on the ground near these plants. Covered by ground litter, the larva pupate in a silk cocoon and emerge the following spring as black caterpillars with two rows of yellow spots along their sides. Look for these gentle butterflies in Hollowell Park and on the alpine tundra.

CHECKERED WHITE

Pontia protodice

White and sulphur family (Pieridae)

Quick ID: dull white with dark markings

Wingspan: 1½–2"

Flight Season: May–August

Checkered white butterflies may be seen as early as May at lower elevations in the park, typically on the east side; later in the season they move into the alpine tundra.

MEAD'S SULPHUR

Colias meadii

White and sulphur family (Pieridae)

Quick ID: deep orange above, olive green below, wings pink edged

Wingspan: 1½–2"

Flight Season: July–August

A butterfly of the tundra and subalpine meadows, Mead's sulphurs are often seen lying sideways on the relatively temperate rocky ground as they warm themselves by exposing their wings and body to the penetrating rays of the sun. The caterpillars feed on alpine clovers such as Parry's clover and whiproot clover, so watch for females laying eggs on these small plants. This fast-flying high-altitude butterfly is named for Theodore Mead, a civil engineer from New York who in 1868 joined a surveying expedition to Colorado to study butterflies.

TIGER SALAMANDER

Ambystoma tigrinum

Mole salamander family (Ambystomidae)

Quick ID: variable coloration—green, yellow or gray with black or yellow dots, bars, or lines

Length: 6–13⅜"

A giant of the salamander world, the tiger salamander is the largest land salamander in North America. Measuring about a foot long and weighing about thirty-three ounces, this goliath has a big appetite that it satisfies with a variety of prey, including worms, insects, mice, and other amphibians. Tiger salamanders live in underground burrows most of the year. In spring breeding season they can be seen at night around ponds and wetlands. Females lay their eggs on vegetation around ponds. In about five months, the larvae metamorphose into adults. Some adults may retain their external gills in the aquatic larval form their entire lives. Look for tiger salamanders in the shallow waters at Lily Lake.

BOREAL TOAD

Bufo boreas

Toad family (Bufonidae)

Quick ID: gray, green or brown; warty; light stripe down middle of back; dark blotches

Length: 2¼–4⅓"

A toad of great distinction, the boreal toad has attracted the attention of many amphibian lovers. In Colorado, the numbers of boreal toads have declined so dramatically since the 1970s that it was placed on the Endangered Species List for the state in 1993. These and other amphibians are battling a spreading disease caused by a chytrid fungus. Boreal toads are high-altitude residents of marshes, alpine meadows and subalpine spruce-fir-forest lakes and streams. Depending on temperatures, they breed from May to July, but unlike most western toads this subspecies has no vocal sac; therefore, their mating call is only a soft chirp. Protected within the boundaries of Rocky Mountain National Park, the status of this endangered toad is being carefully monitored by park biologists.

BOREAL CHORUS FROG

Pseudacris maculata

Treefrog family (Hylidae)

Quick ID: small, pointed snout; dark mask on face; 3 lateral stripes on back

Length: ¾–1½" Weight: .2 oz

A tiny frog with a big voice, boreal chorus frogs are easily heard but not easily seen. Their call rises in pitch and speed as it proceeds, like a comb being drawn from the big teeth to the little teeth. Biologists study population trends of these and other frogs, as they are valuable in determining the health of the ecosystem. Their thin skin is permeable to toxins and contaminants, which makes them critical indicator species of the effects of pollution. The boreal chorus frog is the most abundant and most widely distributed amphibian in Rocky Mountain National Park. Sheep Lakes is a great place to hear these vibrant songsters both day and night.

WESTERN TERRESTRIAL GARTER SNAKE

Thamnophis elegans
Colubrid family (Colubridae)
Quick ID: brown, greenish, or gray; dull-yellow or brown narrow back stripe
Length: 17–41"

The only snake found within the borders of Rocky Mountain National Park, the western terrestrial garter snake is a harmless snake that is rarely seen. There are several subspecies of the western terrestrial garter snake found throughout the western states. The subspecies found in the park is the wandering garter snake, *T. e. vagrans.* Although garter snakes spend most of their time on land, the wandering garter snake may swim in water to avoid predators. They are not picky eaters and will take a variety of food including worms, small fish, slugs, and mice. Considered nonvenomous, recent studies on these snakes have found them to contain mild glandular proteins to help them digest their prey. While hard to spot they are most likely to be found in the lower elevations areas of the park.

BROWN TROUT

Salmo trutta

Salmon and trout family (Salmonidae)

Quick ID: black spots, red spots with blue halos, unspotted tail

Length: 10-16" Weight: 1–2 lb

Native to Europe, brown trout, or brownies as they are commonly called, were introduced into the west for sport fishing. These voracious predators compete with other fish, and declines of native trout species are common where these fish are found. Secretive, they favor areas with overhanging vegetation, undercut banks and submerged snags and rocks. Fishing is allowed in certain streams and lakes in the park but specific rules apply. Please see the park website or ask at one of the park visitor centers or ranger stations for specific regulations.

EASTERN BROOK TROUT

Salvelinus fontinalis

Salmon and trout family (Salmonidae)

Quick ID: dark olive-brown back, silvery belly, pale spots on side, red spots with blue rings, wavy lines (vermiculations) on back and head

Length: 15–20" Weight: 2.2–13.2 lb

Along with rainbow and brown trout, eastern brook trout were introduced as game fish into Rocky Mountain National Park in the 1800s. These nonnative fish outcompete native Colorado trout such as the greenback cutthroat trout and have taken over many of the habitats and niches that they once naturally occupied in the park's mountain streams and lakes. Trout have either dark backgrounds with light markings or light backgrounds with dark markings. Look for these trout spawning in late summer or fall in Sprague Lake.

GREENBACK CUTTHROAT TROUT

Oncorhynchus clarki stomias

Salmon and trout family (Salmonidae)

Quick ID: red stripe on side of throat, round dark spots on sides and tail

Length: 10–15" Weight: 1–4 lb

Thought to be extinct by 1937, the greenback cutthroat trout was rediscovered in the 1950s and listed as an endangered species. With help from biologists, the greenback cutthroat trout was saved from probable extinction as a subspecies. In 1978, the greenback's status in the state was changed to "threatened." This long-forgotten fish is now honored as the state fish of Colorado. The name cutthroat comes from the blood-red slashes on the throat under the jaw. During spawning in gravel shallows, the entire belly may turn a brilliant red. The park's removal of brook trout from the greenbacks' native habitat has been key to their survival. Look for these special trout in park lakes such as Lily, Fern, and Bear Lakes.

RAINBOW TROUT

Oncorhynchus mykiss

Salmon and trout family (Salmonidae)

Quick ID: small, black spots; pinkish stripe on sides and cheeks

Length: 12–18" Weight: 1–3 lb

This popular spring-spawning game fish was introduced from the west coast into park waters to support the casts of anglers. Unfortunately, these and the brown trout outcompete native trout, including the threatened Colorado greenback cutthroat trout. The rainbow trout has dense black specks on its body and most fins, and its tail is heavily spotted. The colorful pinkish stripes on its sides and cheeks give rise to the name rainbow trout.

Key Features of Trout in Rocky Mountain National Park	
Trout Species	**Description**
Brown	Large, dense, black and red spots from tail to head with some on gill covers
Brook	Red spots with blue halos on sides as well as light spots (top side are wavy); fins edged with white
Greenback Cutthroat	Large, sparse, black spots mostly at rear with very few on head
Rainbow	Small, dense, black spots from tail to top of head with none on gill covers

ROCKY MOUNTAIN MAPLE

Acer glabrum

Maple family (Aceraceae)

Quick ID: toothed, lobed leaves; clustered greenish-yellow flowers; smooth gray bark

Height: 20–30'

Visitors from the Eastern states may not recognize the only species of maple in the park, Rocky Mountain maple, as a member of the maple family. Unlike the tall, well-formed trees found in the east, Rocky Mountain maple often has many stems and appears as a large shrub. The paired fruits, called samaras, are attached in a winged shaped V that allows the falling seeds to twirl like a helicopter as they are dispersed from the parent tree. In spring, American Indians used the sweet inner bark to make wine. The strong wood was used to make a variety of tools and furniture such as bows, arrows, snowshoes, fishing net hoops, and cradle frames. You can see this tree along the Lumpy Ridge Trail and Old Fall River Road.

THINLEAF ALDER

Alnus incana spp. *tenuifolia*
Birch family (Betulaceae)
Quick ID: alternate, toothed, 2–4 inch long leaves; flowers are conelike catkins; smooth grayish bark
Height: 12–36'

Thinleaf alder forms thickets often growing with water birch along wet areas including Sprague Lake. Unlike the cones of water birch, alder cones are woody and persistent, remaining year-round on the branches. Root nodules contain nitrogen-fixing bacteria that allow the trees to live in nitrogen poor soils. Thinleaf alder bark was made into a tea for use as a laxative and to relieve hemorrhoids.

WATER BIRCH

Betula occidentalis

Birch family (Betulaceae)

Quick ID: ovate, pointed, 1–2" long leaves; 1–1.5" long catkins; lined reddish brown bark

Height: 12–36'

Also known as river birch or mountain birch, water birch is a small tree or shrub common along montane streams and lakes in the park. Birds such as finches feast on the dry seeds that make up the cylindrical fruit that is called a catkin. Catkins look like small cones, but they break apart. The leaves are abruptly pointed in water birch. American Indians used the strong, flexible wood of birch trees to build shelters. The bark was also used to make canoes, cradles, and baskets.

ROCKY MOUNTAIN JUNIPER

Juniperus scopulorum

Cypress family (Cupressaceae)

Quick ID: small, scalelike needles; green or dark blue berrylike cones; brown to gray scaly bark

Height: 16–49'

The Rocky Mountain juniper is a small shrubby tree with flat, scalelike needles. A small gray bird called Townsend's solitaire (see the Birds chapter) may defend its territory boldly from the top of this evergreen tree, fiercely guarding the pea-sized, fleshy, blueberrylike cones. This bird may have even tried to frighten off American Indians who gathered the berries and branches for many uses including remedies for fevers, colds, sore throats, and even dandruff. This aromatic tree grows in rocky cliff areas or along hillsides in the lower elevations of the park. Rocky Mountain juniper is common in the Lumpy Ridge area at the trailhead to Gem Lake.

COLORADO BLUE SPRUCE

Picea pungens

Pine family (Pinaceae)

Quick ID: bluish green, 1" long needles; downward-hanging, 3–5" long cones; reddish brown scaly bark

Height: 70–115'

The state tree of Colorado, the blue spruce has single, inch-long bluish-green needles with four angles. On all spruce, when the sharp needles fall off, woody pegs remain on the twig, causing a rough appearance. Found at lower elevations in Rocky Mountain National Park, Colorado blue spruce provides protective covering for small owls, while birds such as mountain chickadees and ruby-crowned kinglets glean insects from the trees. A tiny insect called the Cooley spruce gall adelgid, *Adelgis cooleyi,* causes the tree to grow harmless galls that look like small cones at the end of twigs. The adelgid can also inhabit Douglas-fir. The female cones are palm-size on Colorado blue spruce; those of Engelmann spruce are finger-size.

ENGELMANN SPRUCE

Picea engelmannii

Pine family (Pinaceae)

Quick ID: dark green, ¾" long needles; downward-hanging, 2" long cones; light brown bark with loose scales

Height: 75–100'

Bearing the name of George Engelmann (1809–1884), a German physician and botanist, Engelmann spruce is a tall, straight tree with a spire-like crown. Similar in appearance to Colorado blue spruce, Engelmann spruce has smaller cones and four-sided needles that are not as sharp to the touch. Along with subalpine fir, Engelmann spruce is the dominant tree in the subalpine region, growing at elevations of 9,000 to 11,500 feet. Very slow growing, this tree can live more than 300 years. Along with subalpine fir, it grows in a wind-stunted form called "krummholz" at the tree line where the alpine tundra begins. The resonant quality of Engelmann spruce wood is prized for making guitars, violins, and pianos. It was also used by early settlers as a tea and for medicinal purposes.

LIMBER PINE

Pinus flexilis

Pine family (Pinaceae)

Quick ID: 1.5–2.5" long needles; downward-hanging, 5" long cones; gray brown, scaly bark

Height: 35–50'

The limber pine is named for its tough, flexible branches, which help it bend without breaking under the pressure of deep snow. Its twigs are so flexible they can be fashioned into knots. Its long, three-sided evergreen needles grow in bundles of five. A tree of the subalpine region, limber pine can withstand the sustained winds of exposed areas at timberline, but the severe conditions shape them into gnarled, gnomelike, distorted shapes. Look for limber pine along Trail Ridge Road.

LODGEPOLE PINE

Pinus contorta

Pine family (Pinaceae)

Quick ID: 1–3" long needles in bundles of 2; 2" long cones with raised rounded scales thin, scaly bark

Height: 20–80'

Found in thick stands, tall, slender lodgepole pines are found in the park from about 8,000 to 10,500 feet. The twisted, sharply pointed needles grow in pairs. The strong, straight timbers of lodgepole pines were once used as building poles for American Indian teepees. Adapted to forest fires, the cones often remain closed on the trees for many years until high heat from a forest fire causes them to open and drop their tightly held seeds to the ground where they can sprout and regenerate the forest. This type of heat-exposed seed-release cone is called a "serotinous" cone. Recent infestations of mountain pine beetles have caused massive destruction in lodgepole pine forests.

PONDEROSA PINE

Pinus ponderosa

Pine family (Pinaceae)

Quick ID: 3–7" long needles in bundles of 3; egg-shaped cones 3–4" long; red-orange bark

Height: 40–100'

If the aroma of sugar cookies greets you as you hike through the park's forests, look around you for a ponderosa pine, whose bark smells somewhat like cooking vanilla. The bark is thick and reddish orange in color, with furrows between its flat, scaly plates. Apparently tasty, the inner bark was used by American Indians as chewing gum. Abert's squirrels and chickarees relish the seeds held within the cones, which are egg-shaped, with short spines on the scales. Large tracts of Ponderosa pine can be found in the east side of the park.

ROCKY MOUNTAIN DOUGLAS-FIR

Pseudotsuga menziesii

Pine family (Pinaceae)

Quick ID: flat, 1" long needles; 2–3½" long cones; furrowed reddish brown bark

Height: 80–120'

Also known as common Douglas-fir or simply "Doug-fir," the branches of this conifer are long and droopy, giving the tree its pyramidal shape. The name is misleading, as the Douglas-fir is more closely related to hemlocks than to firs. The unique three-pointed bracts that stick out of the downward-hanging cones are helpful in distinguishing this tree from other conifers. An American Indian story associates the bracts with the tail and hind feet of a mouse that ran into the cone to hide from a fox. Found in the forested areas of the park including Wild Basin and Endovalley, the seeds of Douglas-firs are eaten by mice, chipmunks, and squirrels. Clark's nutcrackers cache the seeds in the thick bark and the unretrieved seeds play an important role in the establishment of new trees.

SUBALPINE FIR

Abies lasiocarpa

Pine family (Pinaceae)

Quick ID: soft flat, 1" long needles; purple erect cones 2½–4" long; silvery bark with pimples

Height: 50–80'

The slender, spirelike crowns of subalpine firs form distinctive spears that pierce the crisp blue skies of the subalpine region of the park. Along horizontal branches, the spirally arranged white-lined needles always point upward. Resin covers young purple cones, but disintegrates as they ripen leaving the central spikelike axis behind. Braving extreme wind and cold, these and Engelmann spruce are sometimes wind-beaten into a flag-like appearance, with branches only growing on the side away from the wind. They also take the form of the deformed dwarfed trees in what are known as *krummholz,* which is German for "crooked wood."

BEBB WILLOW

Salix bebbiana

Willow family (Salicaceae)

Quick ID: 1–2.5" long egg-shaped leaves; flowers in 1–2" long catkins; diamond patterned bark

Height: 12–36'

Bebb willow, or Bebb's willow, is named for a botanist from Ohio, Michael Schuck Bebb, who studied willows in the late 1800s. Also known as long-beaked willow and gray willow this shrubby tree forms willow thickets along streamsides and in moist, well-drained areas such as those in Horseshoe Park, where it is heavily grazed by deer and elk. The bark has diamond-shaped patterns on the trunk caused by a fungus. The creative patterns are sought for carvings for furniture, canes, and candleholders. American Indians twisted the bark into ropes and used it to make baskets. The stems were used to make bows and arrows.

NARROWLEAF COTTONWOOD

Populus angustifolia

Willow family (Salicaceae)

Quick ID: 0.5–1" long lance shaped leaves; flowers in 1.5–4" long catkins; furrowed gray bark

Height: 45–60'

Sometimes mistaken as a willow, the leaves of narrowleaf cottonwood are very similar in shape and size to those of most willows. The lance-shaped leaves are about four times longer than wide, and the leaf stalks are less than one-third-inch long. Distinguishing this tree from willows are their sticky, balsam-scented buds, which were used as chewing gum by American Indians. In spring, the female flowers produce clouds of cottony seeds that float through the air like cotton puffs. This and other cottonwood species provide habitat for many species of animals, including beaver, which also use it as a food plant.

QUAKING ASPEN

Populus tremuloides

Willow family (Salicaceae)

Quick ID: 1–3" long heart-shaped leaves; flowers in 1–3" long catkins; smooth whitish gray bark

Height: 40–75'

The quaking aspen, or trembling aspen, has top-flattened, thin flexible stems that move with the slightest breeze, causing its broad leaves to quiver. In autumn, they are a bright golden yellow color. Many types of wildlife make use of aspens including sapsuckers, swallows, bluebirds, warbling vireos, and wrens, sometimes all nesting in the same tree. Elk feed on the bark, twigs, and foliage, causing dark scars on the bark. The long-term experimental enclosures in the park protect stands of aspen from damage by wildlife. Aspen roots spread laterally underground and produce vertical shoots, called suckers. Genetically identical to the parent tree, the young shoots grow into clones, with many members sharing the same root system. Enjoy the aspens along Alberta Falls Trail, Endovalley and many other areas of the park.

BIG SAGEBRUSH

Artemisia tridentate

Aster family (Asteraceae)

Quick ID: greenish blue-gray leaves; creamy yellow flowers; dry, inconspicuous fruit

Height: 6–12'

High in nutrients, sagebrush is used as winter browse by deer, moose, elk, and bighorn sheep. The pungent odor of sagebrush is derived from flammable volatile oils. Widely used by American Indians, the bark was made into baskets and ropes and used as a moccasin liner in winter. The leaves served as a deodorizer and disinfectant in items such as moccasins. Dried, powdered leaves were used on rashes or as baby powder. The Indians also used the leaves in a tea to treat nasal congestion and indigestion and boiled them for use as poultices for wounds, cuts, or sores. Revered as a good luck charm, the leaves were thought to prevent encounters with ghosts. Big sagebrush can be easily seen at the East Inlet Trailhead.

CREEPING OREGON GRAPE

Mahonia repens

Barberry family (Berberidaceae)

Quick ID: hollylike leaves; yellow flowers; blue fruit

Height: 1–3'

April through June, brilliant yellow flowers of creeping Oregon grape brighten forested areas. The "grapes" which follow in late summer are actually berries that are favored by birds and other wildlife. American Indians also used the tart blue berries to make treats such as desserts, jams, and refreshing teas and cold drinks. They also used the roots for many medicinal purposes, such as treating coughs, cleaning wounds and boils, and to ease stomach ailments. The roots also produced a brilliant yellow dye that was used to color baskets and clothing. Please save these berries for the wildlife in the park that depend on the natural resources. Sprague Lake picnic area and East Inlet Trail are good places to see this shrub.

DWARF BIRCH

Betula nana

Birch family (Betulaceae)

Quick ID: glossy round 1–2.5" leaves; flowers in ½" long catkins; reddish bark

Height: 1–6.5'

Of the two species of birch in the park, dwarf birch is the smallest, reaching only shrub size. Also known as bog birch, it is a common plant in wet areas and along streams, including those in Endovalley. The multiple branches spread out, supporting the leathery, toothed leaves that turn scarlet red in autumn. Dwarf birch is important as cover for wildlife, including birds, fish, and mammals. The leaves and twigs are eaten by deer, elk, and moose. This species is also known as *B. glandulosa.*

BRACTED HONEYSUCKLE

Lonicera involucrata

Honeysuckle family (Caprifoliaceae)

Quick ID: opposite oval 2–6" long leaves; paired tubular yellow flowers; round, black berries

Height: 2–6'

Perhaps a more descriptive name for bracted honeysuckle is the common name, black twinberry, as it is the fruit of this shrub that commands attention. In late summer, an eye-catching pair of black berries shine beneath a papery cap of crimson bracts under the oval leaves. Preceding the berries, lovely tubular yellow flowers attract hummingbirds and bees that pollinate the plant. The berries are bitter and cause vomiting. This shrub can be found forming thickets in moist wooded areas such as Wild Basin.

RED ELDERBERRY

Sambucus racemosa var. racemosa

Honeysuckle family (Caprifoliaceae)

Quick ID: compound pinnate leaves; creamy white flowers; red berries (drupes)

Height: 8–20'

Also called red-berried elder, the large clusters of creamy white flowers of red elderberry bloom in June, attracting butterflies and hummingbirds. After the soft pith was pushed out, the hollow elderberry twig could be fashioned into a flute or used as a blowgun toy by American Indian children. The berries of red elderberry contain toxins and were only used occasionally as a food source by American Indians. American Indians used an infusion of the bark and roots to induce vomiting or as a powerful laxative. Red elderberry can be seen in the montane and subalpine zones of the park including along the Green Mountain trailhead and the Wild Basin area.

SNOWBERRY

Symphoricarpos oreophilus

Honeysuckle family (Caprifoliaceae)

Quick ID: 1" round to elliptic leaves; tubular pinkish flowers; white berry

Height: 1–2'

The unusual white berries of this shrub give it the common name snowberry. Also known as mountain snowberry, buckbrush, or waxberry, the small, waxy white berries are apparent in fall and stay on the bush through the winter. They grow well on slopes and along roadsides in open areas such as Beaver Meadows. Considered to have sacred powers, the plant was used to guard against spirits or ghosts. The berries are toxic if eaten in large quantities.

DWARF BLUEBERRY

Vaccinium cespitosum

Heath family (Ericaceae)

Quick ID: alternate 2" long oval leaves; pink, bell-shaped flowers; blue berries

Height: 2–20"

This dwarf blueberry also is called bilberry or huckleberry. Its oval leaves are about 2 inches long with tiny teeth on the margins. The branches are round, and the roots are fibrous. Dwarf blueberry is a low-spreading shrubs especially common in timberline regions and can be readily seen along Trail Ridge Road. Humans have long relished the blue berries, but visitors are asked to leave them for the birds and mammals of the park that rely on them as an important food source.

GROUSE WHORTLEBERRY

Vaccinium scoparium

Heath family (Ericaceae)

Quick ID: pale green ½" long leaves; urn-shaped pink flowers; red berries

Height: 3–8"

Resembling small whisk brooms, the plants form a thick ground cover in mature montane forests. This small shrub is also known as broom huckleberry, grouse huckleberry, littleleaf huckleberry, or bilberry. Although tiny and tedious to harvest, the berries were collected by American Indians and early settlers. Along with another huckleberry, *V. myrtillus,* and the dwarf blueberry, *V. cespitosum,* the berries of grouse whortleberry were made into jams, jellies, and wine. "Whortle" is a derived from the Anglo Saxon word *wyrtil,* which means "a small shrub." The word huckleberry derives from the Middle English slang for "person of little consequence." Grouse whortleberry is easy to see along the roadsides and trails from the Lake Irene area to the park's west entrance at Grand Lake.

KINNIKINNICK

Arctostaphylos uva-ursi

Heath family (Ericaceae)

Quick ID: spoon-shaped leaves; bell-shaped pink leaves; bright red berries

Height: 6–12"

A spreading low-lying shrub with delightful common names, kinnikinnick is also known as bearberry. The word "kinnikinnick" comes from an Algonquian word that means "that which is mixed." Traditionally, the leaves were dried and mixed with other plants, including tobacco, to be smoked. Leaves were also used medicinally to treat a variety of ailments, especially urinary disorders. Additionally, its astringent properties were used as a relieving soak for those suffering from hemorrhoids. Although edible, the bright red berries (drupes) are dry and mealy. The berries often remain on the branches into winter months when they are used by wildlife such as grouse, turkey, deer, elk, and other small mammals.

WAX CURRANT

Ribes cereum

Currant family (Grossulariaceae)

Quick ID: glossy toothed fan-shaped leaves; tubular pink flowers; sticky red berries

Height: 1–3'

Adorned with delightful pink tubular flowers in spring, wax current is a thornless rounded shrub that is very common in ponderosa pine forests on the east side of the park. Even though they are dry and seedy, birds and small mammals ravish the shiny red berries of late summer. When crushed, the alternate glossy, fan-shaped leaves give off a pleasant spicy fragrance. Currants are used for making jams and desserts. American Indians ate the fruit fresh or dried it for use in winter. The species name *cereum* means "waxy," referring to the glossy leaves. Look for this common shrub at Aspenglen Campground and near the Fall River Visitor Center.

WHITESTEM GOOSEBERRY

Ribes inerme

Currant family (Grossulariaceae)

Quick ID: lobed leaves; pinkish white flowers; smooth bluish purple berries

Height: 1–3.5'

The genus *Ribes* includes currants and gooseberries, of which there are 120 species in North and South America. Gooseberries were so named from the custom of stuffing a goose with the berries to add extra flavor during the cooking process. Also known as mountain gooseberry, whitestem gooseberry grows on moist ground, especially along streams, including those in Beaver Meadows. It has one to three spines at the nodes where the leaves are attached along its grayish-white stems. The tart berries are used to make juices, pies, and jams as well as eaten fresh.

WAXFLOWER

Jamesia americana

Hydrangea family (Hydrangeaceae)

Quick ID: ridged leaves with serrated margins; 5-petalled white flowers; dry seedy capsule fruits

Height: 3–6'

In May and June, showy clusters of waxflower decorate roadsides such as Old Fall River Road with fragrant, white five-petaled flowers. Growing up to 6 feet tall and 4 to 6 feet wide, this shrub adds a pleasant fragrance to the spring air. In fall the leaves turn orange and pink, creating a pleasant splash of color to the hillsides. Sometimes called cliffbush or Jamesia, the shrub was named to honor Edwin James, the botanist who traveled with Stephen Long on the discovery expedition of 1820 that helped explore and map the land obtained in the Louisiana Purchase from France.

AMERICAN RED RASPBERRY

Rubus idaeus

Rose family (Rosaceae)

Quick ID: 3 to 5 leaflets; white flowers; red berries

Height: 3–5'

A familiar shrub, the American red raspberry provides nutritious, sweet berries for humans and wildlife. Also known as wild red raspberry, the plant has stems with prickles and stiff, straight hairs that make collecting the berries a painful process for people, but not for the birds and other wildlife that rely on these fruits as a fall energy source. This plant was used extensively by American Indians for a variety of ailments, including diarrhea, menstrual problems, and to ease childbirth. These shrubs often grow on rocky hillsides and can be see along Old Fall River Road.

ANTELOPE BITTERBRUSH

Purshia tridentata

Rose family (Rosaceae)

Quick ID: 3-lobed leaves; creamy yellow flowers; slender leathery fruit

Height: 3–16'

Antelope bitterbrush is known by several common names including antelope brush or bitterbrush. An important food plant for mule deer in the park, it is often heavily browsed into a low, spreading shrub. The creamy yellow blossoms are pleasantly scented, and their aroma sweetens the air in May and June. The wedge-shaped leaves have three rounded lobes on the tip. The roots were used medicinally by American Indians for coughs and fevers. This is one of the plants collected by Lewis and Clark during their western expedition of 1804 to1806. Look for this shrub in ponderosa pine forests and open hillsides in the park.

BOULDER RASPBERRY

Rubus deliciosus

Rose family (Rosaceae)

Quick ID: 3–5 lobed leaves; flat white flowers; dark red berries

Height: 1–4'

Boulder raspberry was first collected near Boulder, Colorado, by Edwin James, who was a botanist on the 1820 Stephen Long expedition to explore the newly acquired land of the Louisiana Purchase. The large white flowers of Boulder raspberry resemble flat, white roses, but the arching stems lack the thorns of true roses or the spines of other raspberries. The 1.5-to-2-inch wide leaves are crinkled and have three to five lobes. In fall, the dark purplish red berry is seedy and dry but is an important source of nutrients for birds and mammals. Raspberries such as black raspberry contain pigments called anthocyanins, which have been shown to inhibit cancers. Look for these shrubs in the Beaver Meadows area.

CHOKECHERRY

Prunus virginiana

Rose family (Rosaceae)

Quick ID: toothed oval leaves; white flowers; blue-black fruit

Height: 12–30'

Highly prized, chokecherry is one of the most important plants for wildlife and historically for American Indians. Sometimes forming thickets, this large shrub often reaches 20 to 30 feet in height. In spring it is covered with white bottle-brush blooms which are replaced by clusters of blue-black berries in fall. The fruit and leaves are browsed by large mammals, including bears, moose, bighorn sheep, and deer. Small mammals and birds also enjoy the fruits, which are high in vitamins and minerals. The Arapaho mashed the berries, formed them into patties, and dried the berry patties to be used throughout the winter. The inner bark was made into a medicinal tea to stop diarrhea. The name chokecherry refers to "choking" or "plugging" the effects of diarrhea.

SASKATOON SERVICEBERRY

Amelanchier alnifolia

Rose family (Rosaceae)

Quick ID: alternate oval leaves; star-shaped white flowers; dark purple berries

Height: 12–30'

Not only is the Saskatoon serviceberry prized for its many uses, but it also adds ornamental beauty to the forests of Rocky Mountain National Park. In spring, the white star-shaped blossoms burst out like popcorn, covering the branches. In fall, the leaves turn yellow to reddish as the purple berries adorn the plant. Elk, deer, moose, and bighorn sheep browse the tender stems and leaves. The nutritious berry-like fruits called drupes were cooked in a variety of foods and used to make a purple dye. American Indians used the strong branches to shape arrows, spears, and pipe stems.

SHRUBBY CINQUEFOIL

Dasiphora fruticosa ssp. *floribunda*
Rose family (Rosaceae)
Quick ID: divided leaflets; yellow buttercuplike flowers; hairy fruits
Height: 2–4'

Like a shrub full of buttercups, shrubby cinquefoil brightens the roadsides and open areas in summer. The name cinquefoil is derived from a French word meaning five-leaf, referring to the five fingerlike leaflets on many of these plants. The Latin name of this shrub has been undergoing systematic changes, and synonyms include *Potentilla fruticosa, Pentaphylloides floribunda,* and *Dasiphora floribunda,* all of which refer to the same plant. Common in moist areas throughout the montane and subalpine region of the park, you can look for this shrub along Bear Lake Road and the Sprague Lake area.

WOODS' ROSE

Rosa woodsii

Rose family (Rosaceae)

Quick ID: compound pinnate leaves; pink flowers; seedy rose hip

Height: 3–6'

The rose family boasts about 2,000 members that include not only familiar rosebushes but also trees such as apples, cherries, hawthorns, and serviceberries. Commonly called prairie rose, Woods' rose is found growing in western states from the plains to the subalpine zone. The five-petaled flowers of roses produce the familiar scent meant to attract pollinators. The fleshy red fruits of roses are called "hips." High in vitamin C, rose hips have a uniquely sweet but pleasantly tart flavor. The hips were commonly used for jellies, jams, and syrups by early settlers. The hips were also used medicinally for sore throats and other common ailments by American Indians. Rose leaves were placed in moccasins as a treatment for athlete's foot. The name Woods' rose refers to Joseph Woods, a rose expert.

DIAMONDLEAF WILLOW

Salix planifolia

Willow family (Salicaceae)

Quick ID: oblong 1–2" long leaves; flowers in 1–2" long catkins; shiny reddish-brown bark

Height: 3–13'

One of the sixteen species of willow in the park, diamondleaf willow is also known as planeleaf or tealeaf willow. This small tree or shrub has trunks in clusters and bark that often peels into strips or flakes. The leaves are shiny hairless above; underneath they have a whitish powdery coating called a "bloom" that you can rub off. There are about 120 species of willow in North America and over 300 worldwide. For thousands of years willow bark has been used medicinally to relieve aches and pains and was reportedly used by Lewis and Clark on their expedition of western discovery. Willows are found along streams and in many wet areas of the park.

PARK WILLOW

Salix monticola

Willow family (Salicaceae)

Quick ID: narrow oblong leaves; flower in catkins; fruit is a capsule

Height: 5–19'

Park willow is the tallest and most common willow in the park. It grows in lower elevations up to 9,000 feet. Several other common names include mountain willow, Rocky Mountain willow, cherry willow, and white willow. Forming thickets along stream banks and moist slopes, willows are a vital source of food and shelter for wildlife in the park. Elk, moose, and deer heavily browse the leaves. Birds build their nests in the protective shelter of the thickets. Beaver utilize the branches to build their lodges and dams. Fish often find shade and cover in the overhanging branches. The tough, flexible stems of willows were widely used by American Indians to make baskets, furniture, and arrows, and the bark was medicinally used like aspirin.

SCOULER'S WILLOW

Salix scouleriana

Willow family (Salicaceae)

Quick ID: narrow oblong 1–2.5" long leaves; flowers in 1–2.5" in long catkins; brownish bark
Height: 3–13'

Scouler's willow, or Scouler willow, is named for John Scouler a Scottish naturalist who, from 1824 to 1826, studied and collected many specimens of western plants on an exploratory voyage. Unlike most willows, Scouler's willow can be found not only in wet areas but also on dry hillsides. The flowers on catkins turn the leafless tree into a mass of yellow in the spring. The leaves, whose undersides have flat, reddish hairs, appear after the catkins flower. Look for Scouler's willow along Trail Ridge Road and Bear Lake.

SNOW WILLOW

Salix nivalis

Willow family (Salicaceae)

Quick ID: broadly oval, ½–2" long leaves; flowers are catkins on leafy shoots; silky seeds

Height: 3–4"

With broad, thick, flat leaves that barely reach ankle height, this miniature shrub forms dense mats that lie close to the ground in the subalpine to alpine regions of the park. The other dwarf willow found at this high altitude is alpine willow *(S. petrophila)*. The male and female flowers of willows are borne on separate plants. The cottony hairs on willow seeds act as wind sails, enabling the seeds to float on currents of air to land away from the parent plant. *Salix* is the genus name for all willows. In Latin, the species name *nivalis* means "snow" and *petrophila* means "rock lover."

SHINING WILLOW

Salix lucida

Willow family (Salicaceae)

Quick ID: lancelike, 2–6.5" long leaves; flowers in 1–2" long catkins; reddish brown bark

Height: 12–20'

Growing at lower elevations in the park, the smooth, glossy leaves of shining willow, or greenleaf willow, shimmer and shine in the bright summer sun. This species comprises several subspecies, including *Salix lucida* ssp. *caudata* or *Salix lasiandra* var. *caudata,* sometimes referred to as whiplash willow. Willows were an important plant for American Indians who used the wood and bark for making furniture, structures, baskets, and bows. The leaves were smoked for asthma and used with kinnikinnick as a smoking mixture. The leaves were also used for colds and sore throats.

DOUGLAS-FIR DWARF MISTLETOE

Arceuthobium douglasii

Christmas mistletoe family (Viscaceae)

Quick ID: tiny scaley leaves; tiny greenish yellow flowers; greenish blue berrylike fruits

Height: varies as branches

An unwelcomed guest, mistletoe lives its life without paying a dime in rent, never lifting a finger to help, and never offering to assist with food expenses. Several species of these freeloaders are parasitic on specific evergreen trees, where they embed their long, threadlike roots into the branches of their powerless hosts. The affected trees form weird tufts or growths called witches' brooms. The infestation gradually kills the tree, as the mistletoe saps the nutrients from the crown. Mistletoe seeds are surrounded by a sticky substance, and are often carried on the feet of birds or small mammals. To find mistletoe, look up into forested areas throughout the park for oddly shaped masses of stems on tree branches.

COW PARSNIP

Heracleum maximum

Carrot family (Apiaceae)

Quick ID: large white flowers; large coarsely toothed leaves

Height: 3.5–10' Bloom Season: May–August

Growing in moist, shady areas, especially along park roads and trails, cow parsnip, a giant among flowers, towers above its lowlier neighbors. Sometimes reaching up to ten feet and with broad leaves up to 20 inches across, the genus name *Heracleum,* deriving from Hercules, son of Zeus, suits this flower well. Wildlife, including deer, elk, moose, and bear, eat the flat-topped dinner-plate-size flowers and tender stems of this plant. American Indians peeled the tender young stalks and boiled them in stews. Children used the hollow stems as blowguns and flutes. Medicinally, the leaves were used as a tonic for colds, and mashed roots were applied as a poultice for rheumatism. Look for this plant along Old Fall River Road.

ROCKY MOUNTAIN LOCO

Oxytropis sericea

Pea family (Fabaceae)

Quick ID: white or creamy flowers; 2–12" long leaves with 11–21 leaflets

Height: 6–16" Bloom Season: May–September

From the innocent-looking creamy white blooms to the long taproot, all parts of Rocky Mountain locoweed or whitepoint locoweed are poisonous. Due to an alkaloid called swainsonine, it can cause chronic neurological damage to livestock, deer, and elk that consume it in quantities. Poisoned animals will suffer trembling, paralysis, and blindness. In spite of its undesirable reputation, Rocky Mountain locoweed is one of the first colonizers of fire-damaged areas, and it has the ability to fix atmospheric nitrogen into a useable state. American Indians used an infusion of the leaves for ear problems and to apply to sores. The stems were used by children to make headdresses. It is also the food plant for many butterfly caterpillars. Rocky Mountain loco grows in disturbed areas along roads and meadows.

GUNNISON'S MARIPOSA LILY

Calochortus gunnisonii
Lily family (Liliaceae)
Quick ID: creamy white flowers; long narrow leaves
Height: 8–20" Bloom Season: July–August

From July to August Gunnison's mariposa lily, or sego lily, blooms in Rocky Mountain National Park in open meadows at lower elevations such as the Beaver Meadows area. The creamy-white bowl-shaped petals resemble the wings of a butterfly; hence the name mariposa, which in Spanish means "butterfly." In July, look for these delicate lilies in open meadows, including those at the Beaver Meadows Entrance Station. This lily was named to honor the mid-1800s western explorer Captain J.W. Gunnison. American Indians dried the bulbs and stored them to cook as porridge in the winter. They used an infusion from the plant to reduce swelling from rheumatism. It also may have helped them win horse races, as the root was placed into a horse's mouth before a race.

AMERICAN BISTORT

Bistorta bistortoides

Buckwheat family (Polygonaceae)

Quick ID: white flowers; long lance-like leaves

Height: 8–28" Bloom Season: June–August

The small white flower heads of American bistort dot the meadows of Rocky Mountain National Park like hundreds of cotton balls atop tall, thin reddish stems. Sometimes the white flowers have a pink tinge to them, adding subtle color to green meadows during the summer. The roots of bistort were widely used by American Indians like potatoes. They baked the chestnut-flavored roots or cooked them in soups and stews. They also dried the seeds, which they then ground into flour for bread. The genus was recently changed from *Polygonum* to *Bistorta.*

ALPINE SUNFLOWER

Tetraneuris grandiflora

Aster family (Asteraceae)

Quick ID: large yellow daisylike flowers; narrow woolly leaves

Height: 3–8"   Bloom Season: July–August

With bright yellow flower heads up to four inches across, the alpine sunflower is one of the superstars of the tundra. The dense hairs that cover the short stem and feathery leaves help protect the plant from the near-constant wind and intense rays of the sun. These soft white hairs give rise to the common name, old man of the mountain. The alternate Latin name, *Rydbergia grandiflora,* honors a Swedish botanist Per Axel Rydberg, who wrote the first *Flora of the Rocky Mountains.* The genus name *grandiflora* means large flower, which aptly describes this big-headed dwarfed sunflower. Look for these bright flowers along Tundra Communities Trail, Alpine Ridge Trail and Ute Trail but please leave them for others to enjoy.

HEART-LEAVED ARNICA

Arnica cordifolia

Aster family (Asteraceae)

Quick ID: yellow daisylike flowers; opposite heart-shaped leaves

Height: 12–24" Bloom Season: June–August

As the name suggests, its lower heart-shaped leaves give this flower its descriptive name. Its bright yellow flowers resemble sunflowers, but on arnicas, the leaves are positioned oppositely on the stem while the leaves of most sunflowers are positioned alternately. Long used medicinally for swellings, strains, and bruises, the plant can cause blistering if applied to broken skin or mucus membranes. Due to the heartlike shape of the leaves, this plant was also believed to have magical powers. American Indians mixed the dried roots with a powered dye and painted the mixture on their face. The name of a desired person was then recited assuring the user of true love.

MOUNTAIN GUMWEED
Grindelia subalpina
Aster family (Asteraceae)
Quick ID: yellow daisylike flowers; alternate toothed leaves
Height: 8–18"   Bloom Season: July–September

True to its name, gumweeds are indeed gummy due to a sticky resin on their stems and leaves. Their flower buds are also gummy, covered with a gooey white sap which helps protect the developing flowers from insect invaders until they are ready for pollination. Gumweeds were used by American Indians to treat colds and coughs, bronchitis, and asthma. The flower heads were used to relieve the incessant itch of poison ivy and as a salve for wounds and rashes. Blooming in midsummer, the bright yellow flowers are commonly seen along roadsides and on montane slopes.

GOLDEN BANNER

Thermopsis divaricarpa

Pea family (Fabaceae)

Quick ID: bright yellow flowers; leaves with 3 leaflets

Height: 1–3' Bloom Season: May–July

Tall bright yellow blooms of golden banner greet visitors to the park. Common along the park's roadways, meadows, and hillsides, this widespread plant, also called golden pea, is similar in appearance to lupines, except that it has three leaflets on each leaf while lupines have at least five. Found in dry open areas, golden banner flowers are composed of five petals, including an upper petal called the banner and two adjacent petals that resemble wings. The two bottom petals are fused and form a structure that resembles the keel on a boat. After blooming, seeds form in pods; these are poisonous and should be avoided. Like other members of the pea family, golden banner is an important source of nitrogen fixation in the soil.

PINEDROPS

Pterospora andromedea

Indian-pipe family (Monotropaceae)

Quick ID: pale yellow bell-shaped flowers; leaves are narrow scales

Height: 1–4' Bloom Season: June–August

An oddity among the wildflower world, pinedrops occasionally catch the eye of hikers in the rich woodlands of the park. Its reddish-brown stems blend well with the dappled forest light, creating camouflage for the plant, which can reach 4 feet in height. Tiny, yellow bell-shaped flowers hang down from the top of the plant's stem, which is covered with a sticky substance. The stem becomes woody when dry and often remains standing throughout the winter season. Pinedrops lack chlorophyll and are reliant on the roots of conifers and a soil fungus to provide nourishment. Pinedrops may not bloom consistently. Look for them in rich ponderosa woodlands including the Wild Basin area.

ALPINE AVENS

Geum rossii ssp. *turbinatum*
Rose family (Rosaceae)
Quick ID: yellow flowers; fernlike leaves with overlapping toothed leaflets
Height: 2–6" Bloom Season: July–August

Blooming quickly in the short summer months, masses of shiny yellow buttercuplike flowers brighten the tundra. Alpine avens, or Ross' avens, are found in masses in moist subalpine and alpine meadows in July and August. Many plants produce chemicals to deter herbivores from eating them. Alpine avens produces phenols that make the plant bitter and difficult to digest. The phenols also inhibit microbes from decomposing the plant. Pikas take advantage of this natural preservative and add alpine avens to their stored haystacks to prevent decomposition. Over the long winter, the phenol levels drop, and the plant can be safely eaten by the pikas. You can see alpine avens at Forest Canyon Overlook and the Rock Cut area.

SHOWY MILKWEED

Asclepias speciosa

Milkweed family (Asclepiadaceae)

Quick ID: pinkish-white rounded flowerheads; oblong opposite leaves

Height: 1.5–3' Bloom Season: June–August

Commonly found at lower elevations in Rocky Mountain National Park, showy milkweed can be seen along roadsides and in open fields and meadows. Although all milkweeds are poisonous, showy milkweed is the least toxic, and many parts of the plant were traditionally used as a food source or for medicinal purposes by American Indians. The milky latex in the stems and leaves was used to remove warts, corns, and calluses. The latex was even used as chewing gum. Monarch butterflies lay their eggs on the underside of milkweed leaves. When the caterpillars emerge, they feed on the toxic leaves, incorporating the toxic taste into their bodies, which deters predators such as birds from eating them.

PARRY'S CLOVER

Trifolium parryi

Pea family (Fabaceae)

Quick ID: rosy mauve flower; basal three-parted leaves

Height: 2–6" Bloom Season: June–August

Forming colorful rosy clumps in the subalpine and alpine regions of the park, these miniature beauties are best appreciated sitting down, as the delicate pealike flowers are likely to be overlooked from standing height. This small, fragrant flower is named to honor Charles Christopher Parry (1823–1890), a botanist who came to be known as the "King of Colorado Botany." Parry studied under some of the most well-known names in the world of botany, including Asa Gray, John Torrey, and George Engelmann, all of whom made significant impacts in the discovery and naming of the plants of North America. His extensive plant collections were important in documenting the botanical wonders of Colorado and the area that would become Rocky Mountain National Park.

FIREWEED

Chamerion angustifolium

Evening primrose family (Onagraceae)

Quick ID: rose pink flowers; narrow alternate leaves

Height: 1–10' Bloom Season: June–September

Bright showy clusters of tall rosy-pink flowers line the roads in many areas of Rocky Mountain National Park. Colonizing burned areas, fireweed spreads rapidly, creating waving meadows of beauty where fire recently blackened the earth. The small seeds, encased in erect, slim pods, are supplied with fluffy white hairs that sail the seeds through the air when the pods dry. Elk and deer eat the flowers and stems. American Indians used fireweed, which is high in vitamins, as a nutritious food source, eating young shoots like asparagus and enjoying the flower petals steeped as a drink.

FAIRY SLIPPER

Calypso bulbosa
Orchid family (Orchidaceae)
Quick ID: light pinkish rose flower; single basal oval leaf
Height: 2–9" Bloom Season: May–June

The strikingly beautiful blooms of the fairy slipper orchid never cease to delight the eye when they are found blossoming in moist forested areas from 7,000 to 10,000 feet elevation. The slipper-like lower petal is adorned with bright yellow hairs that attract bees. Bees soon learn, however, that they have been tricked into visiting these gorgeous flowers, as they do not provide any nectar reward. The single oval leaf appears in the fall and remains until early spring but dies away soon after the flower appears. The Latin name *Calypso* refers to the sea nymph of Homer's *Odyssey* and *bulbosa* to the bulblike roots or corms.

SCARLET GILIA

Ipomopsis aggregata

Phlox family (Polemoniaceae)

Quick ID: bright red flowers; divided alternate leaves

Height: 1–4' Bloom Season: July–August

Fairy trumpet is an alternate name used for the striking 1- to 2-inch-long red flowers of scarlet gilia. Scarlet gilia was once placed in the genus *Gilia* but later was moved to *Ipomopsis.* Irresistible to hummingbirds, their tubular red flowers are shaped for these efficient pollinators. Found in fields and meadows throughout the park, these flowers can be seen in July at the Beaver Meadows Visitor Center's native-plant gardens. If you are quiet and patient, you may also get a great look at a broad-tailed or rufous hummingbird as they enjoy the sweet nectar provided by the flowers.

SHOOTING STAR

Dodecatheon pulchellum

Primrose family (Primulaceae)

Quick ID: magenta flowers; basal oblong leaves

Height: 4–24" Bloom Season: June–July

Perched on a tall, thin, leafless stem, the bright magenta petals of shooting star flare backwards and resemble shooting stars. The reddish stamens protrude from the flower like the tip of a missile, attracting bees that pollinate the flowers in a process called buzz-pollination, in which the small insects vibrate their thoracic muscles to shake the pollen from the anthers. American Indians used an infusion of the leaves of shooting star as a gargle for mouth sores and as an eye wash. These colorful, springy lawn darts are abundant in wet meadows and along streams, including those near Lake Irene, Hidden Valley, and Endovalley.

SCARLET PAINTBRUSH

Castilleja miniata

Figwort family (Scrophulariaceae)

Quick ID: red bracts that resemble flowers; alternate linear leaves

Height: 1–2' Bloom Season: June–August

Nature has colored summer in the Rockies with bright splashes of scarlet flowers that are eye-catching against a dark background of green leaves. The plant's actual flowers are hidden behind its colorful red bracts, which attract hummingbirds. Hummingbirds probe the plants with their long slender bills, drinking the sweet nectar inside its tubular flowers. As they move from flower to flower, they pick up pollen and transfer it to the next paintbrush, becoming unknowing but effective pollinators. Paintbrushes come in a wide variety of colors, from red to orange to yellow, and their identification can be challenging due to the large number of species. Look for paintbrushes decorating meadows and waysides throughout the park.

ELEPHANTHEAD

Pedicularis groenlandica

Figwort family (Scrophulariaceae)

Quick ID: pink tiny elephant head shaped flowers; fernlike flowers

Height: 1–2' Bloom Season: June–August

A delightfully whimsical character in the world of wildflowers makes its home in marshy areas of Rocky Mountain National Park. Arising in torchlike clusters of pink blooms, this amusing flower is uniquely named elephanthead or elephantella. If you look closely at the tiny flower, you'll see two floppy petals that resemble ears and a long curved petal that's shaped like the upturned trunk of a little pink elephant, which just happens to be another common name for this flower. Related to snapdragons, this cartoon-character flower can be seen in Big Meadows and along Lake Irene Trail.

BIGELOW'S TANSYASTER

Machaeranthera bigelovii

Aster family (Asteraceae)

Quick ID: lavender daisylike flowers with yellow center; slender, divided leaves

Height: 1–3' Bloom Season: July–September

Blooming in late summer, the lavender daisylike flowers of Bigelow's tansyaster fill the warm meadows with pastel waves of color. Native to western North America, tansyasters are members of the aster family. Colorful, daisylike lavender petals stretch like rays around a button of tiny bright-yellow disk flowers in the center of the bloom. The flattened flower makes an enticing landing pad for pollinators such as bees and butterflies. The flower is named to honor botanist John Bigelow, who collected plant specimens in the west in the mid 1800s. Bigelow's tansyasters can be seen along the roadsides near the Fall River Entrance Station and Moraine Park.

ALPINE FORGET-ME-NOT

Eritrichium nanum

Borage family (Boraginaceae)

Quick ID: Bluish purple flowers with yellow center; hairy silvery leaves

Height: 1–2"   Bloom Season: June–August

The plant life of the alpine tundra (as well as the hikes to see them) can be breathtaking. At over 12,000 feet, a walk along Toll Memorial Trail is one of the easiest places to spot alpine beauties such as the striking alpine forget-me-not. In summer, the short paved trail just off Trail Ridge Road at Rock Cut is bordered with a dazzling show of dense clusters of yellow-eyed sky blue flowers. These small plants are a vital part of the fragile tundra ecosystem. Please stay on the trail and leave the wildflowers for others to enjoy.

TALL FRINGED BLUEBELLS

Mertensia ciliata

Borage family (Boraginaceae)

Quick ID: pink to blue bell-shaped flowers; alternate, broadly lance-shaped leaves

Height: 1–3' Bloom Season: June–August

Dangling gracefully from arching stems, nodding clusters of delicate bell-shaped blue flowers line shaded stream banks in the park. Also known as mountain bluebells or mountain chiming bells, the flower buds are pink with blue tinges and turn blue as they open. Most flowers in the borage family have rough hairs. The name borage comes from the Latin word *burra* which means "rough hairs," but tall chiming bells has smooth leaves with several prominent veins. Another species, lanceleaf chiming bells, *M. lanceolata,* is also found in the park, but it has somewhat hairy leaves with one prominent vein in the leaves. In July, look for bluebells along Bear Lake Trail, Milner Pass, and in Wild Basin along the Ouzel Falls Trail.

MOUNTAIN HAREBELL

Campanula rotundifolia
Harebell family (Campanulaceae)
Quick ID: blue bell-shaped flowers; basal, rounded leaves
Height: 1–3' Bloom Season: June–August

The graceful, slender stems seem barely strong enough to support the large bluebell-shaped flowers of mountain harebell. Common in many mountainous areas of the world, harebells are also called bluebells, bluebell bellflower, common bellflower, and Bluebell-of-Scotland. The bell-like shape of these innocent flowers has led to imaginative beliefs and folklore. The flowers were thought to shelter fairies, and the juice was used as part of a witch's flying ointment. It was also thought to be used by witches to transform themselves into hares to escape detection. American Indians rubbed the plant on their bodies as protection while hunting and also to protect them from witches. Look for harebells along Old Fall River Road.

KING'S CROWN

Rhodiola integrifolia

Stonecrop family (Crassulaceae)

Quick ID: dark purplish red flattened flowers; fleshy leaves are curved upward along the thick stem

Height: 2–12" Bloom Season: June–August

Flattened on the top, its deep maroon flower heads create a miniature crown of regal petals. With thickened stems and succulent leaves, king's crown and its close relatives, queen's crown, *Clementsia rhodantha,* and yellow sedum, *Amerosedum lanceolatum,* are members of the stonecrop family, many of which are able to grow on rocks with a very thin layer of soil. This plant is also known as ledge stonecrop and roseroot. It has undergone a number of name changes including *Sedum rosea* and *S. integrifolium.* The current Latin name *Rhodiola* means "rose-like" and *integrifolia* means "complete foliage." The root has a roselike fragrance. Look for king's crown and its relatives growing on rocky ledges and in subalpine and alpine meadows and near the Alpine Visitor Center and Medicine Bow Curve Overlook.

SILVERY LUPINE

Lupinus argenteus

Pea family (Fabaceae)

Quick ID: blue violet flowers; palm-shaped leaves

Height: 1–3' Bloom Season: June–July

Silvery lupine (pronounced "loop'-in") was one of the nearly 200 plants collected by Lewis and Clarke on their exploratory journey through the west. The park hosts three species of lupine, along with several subspecies that grow throughout the park. The grayish silvery-green leaves and stem give this lupine the name silvery lupine. The blue flowers form large colonies sometimes covering hillsides in a carpet of blue haze. Lupines often grow in dry rocky soils. This characteristic lead to the name "lupine," which means "wolflike" or "ravenous," as it was mistakenly thought that the plants robbed the soil of nutrients. Like most members of the pea family, lupines have root nodules containing nitrogen-fixing bacteria that allow it to deposit nitrogen, which replenishes the soil.

PURPLE FRINGE

Phacelia sericea

Waterleaf family (Hydrophyllaceae)

Quick ID: purple flowers in clustered cylinders; silvery green, hairy lobed leaves

Height: 4–16" Bloom Season: June–August

The vibrant purple flowers of purple fringe, or silky phacelia, are commonly found decorating the alpine tundra. Clustered in cylinders on upright stems, the small flowers project long, conspicuous bristles that resemble miniature clumps of bottlebrushes. The colorful bristles are actually composed of protruding purple stamens and golden yellow anthers that aid the flower in depositing pollen on insects that visit the flowers. Elk dine on these flowers in spring and summer. Found from the montane to alpine region, look for these distinctive clumps of pincushion flowers along Trail Ridge Road and at Lava Cliffs.

ROCKY MOUNTAIN IRIS

Iris missouriensis
Iris family (Iridaceae)
Quick ID: violet-blue flowers; narrow sword-shaped leaves
Height: 1–2' Bloom Season: May–June

Often complemented by the bright yellow flowers of golden banner, the showy blue flowers of Rocky Mountain iris fill the park's moist meadows, creating vibrant seas of spring color. Also known as western blue flag, western iris, or mountain iris, the flower is formed by three blue petals that stand upright and three violet-and-yellow striped sepals that droop downward. These colorful stripes serve as nectar guides to channel pollinators such as bumblebees and hummingbirds into the flowers. The thickened roots, or rhizomes, contain a toxin called irisin, which causes severe vomiting. Used medicinally, the plant was used by American Indians to treat rheumatism, toothaches, and earaches. In early spring, Horseshoe Park is a good place to see these irises.

WILD BERGAMOT

Monarda fistulosa var. *menthaefolia*

Mint family (Lamiaceae)

Quick ID: lavender to pink flowers; opposite, pointed, finely toothed leaves

Height: 2–5' Bloom Season: June–August

For American Indians and early colonists, the fields and forests were living gardens filled with summer bounty, including the gifts of the wild bergamot. In July they gathered and dried the grayish-green leaves for later use as a flavorful minty tea (bergamot is also called horsemint) and as medicine against coughs, colds, and other respiratory problems. They also added wild bergamot as a spice to meats, soups, and stews. Wild bergamot's long tubular flowers are specially suited to attract pollinators such as hummingbirds and butterflies. You can easily see these lovely flowers along the roadsides near Beaver Meadows Visitor Center.

COLORADO COLUMBINE

Aquilegia coerulea

Buttercup family (Ranunculaceae)

Quick ID: delicate light blue flowers; deeply cleft divided leaves

Height: 1–2' Bloom Season: June–August

Often seen growing precariously on overhanging rock ledges, the Colorado columbine is an eye-catching beauty. Well chosen to represent Colorado as the state flower, the delicate but rugged white-and-lavender blossoms are as unique as the state. The flower's five white petals are highlighted by a background of five showy blue sepals. Projecting down from the flower are five long, slender blue spurs that are specially suited to supply hummingbirds with a sweet nectar treat as they transfer pollen to the next flower. In summer look for these fragile flowers growing along Trail Ridge Road, but please leave them for others to enjoy.

PASQUEFLOWER

Pulsatilla patens ssp. *multifida*

Buttercup family (Ranunculaceae)

Quick ID: crocuslike lavender flowers; dusty green fuzzy leaves

Height: 6–12" Bloom Season: May–June

Visitors from lower elevations can experience the joy of a "second" spring as wildflowers bloom later in Rocky Mountain National Park. In the park, high elevations produce lower temperatures, and flowers that brave the cool May temperatures often blossom as the snow is melting around them. Pasqueflowers are one of the earliest bloomers and can be seen along many lower-elevation trails, including Lily Lake Trail and Gem Lake Trail in late May or early June. The silky white hairs covering the stems and sepals of this crocuslike flower help to protect it from the elements. Lacking petals, the highly modified lavender sepals encircle many bright yellow stamens. The flower opens wide on sunny days to quickly attract as many insects as possible to ensure pollination.

ROCKY MOUNTAIN CLEMATIS

Clematis columbiana

Buttercup family (Ranunculaceae)

Quick ID: violet-blue drooping flowers; viney lobed leaves

Height: 6–12' Bloom Season: May–June

Also known as rock clematis, Rocky Mountain clematis is a creeping vine that travels along the ground and climbs eagerly over rocks and other plants. The showy violet-blue sepals are about 2 inches long and look like miniature tents that cover the reproductive parts. The seeds have long silky threads that are dispersed in the winds of autumn. The leaflets are usually deeply lobed. In early spring, look for this pretty vine blooming around the Sprague Lake Trail. In July and August, the tennis-ball-size whitish seed heads are noticeable and appear to be large twisted cottony orbs covering talus slopes, rock walls, and other plants.

ONESIDE PENSTEMON

Penstemon unilateralis

Figwort family (Scrophulariaceae)

Quick ID: bell shaped purple flowers; thin opposite leaves

Height: 24–30" Bloom Season: July–August

The wide mouths of penstemons are a perfect fit for large bees such as this western black and gold bumblebee, *Bombus nevadensis*. The stamens and anthers are strategically positioned to place a bit of pollen on the back of the bee for conveyance to another flower for pollination. Penstemons have five stamens (male structures) but only four of them possess anthers where the pollen is held. The fifth stamen is sterile, flattened at the tip and often bearded, thus the common name "beardtongue." In the park, look for the tall wands of oneside penstemon as well as eight other penstemon species in open sunny areas in meadows and fields and along roadsides, including Old Fall River Road.

Grasses are a vitally important source of food for many animals as well as humans. Grasses have jointed stems, while the stems of sedges and rushes lack joints. The stems of sedges have edges, and those of rushes are round. Sedges and rushes are usually found in areas with high moisture content, such as along streambeds and wetlands.

EBONY SEDGE
Carex ebenea
Sedge family (Cyperaceae)
Quick ID: dark seed heads, grows in tufts

The dark seed heads of ebony sedge give this plant its descriptive name. The stems of most sedges are wedge shaped, and botany students often remember this by saying "sedges have edges." There are about seventy-five species of sedges in the park, and animals such as elk rely heavily on these as an important food source. This high elevation sedge can be seen along Trail Ridge Road and Old Fall River Road.

ALPINE BLUEGRASS

Poa alpina
Grass family (Poaceae)
Quick ID: purplish seed heads

Alpine bluegrass is an important food source for the animals that live at high altitudes in the park such as those near Forest Canyon Overlook.

BLUE GAMMA GRASS

Bouteloua gracilis
Grass family (Poaceae)
Quick ID: seedheads on one side

Resembling fields of miniature flags, blue gamma grass is very distinctive with its seedheads flagging one side of the top of the stem. Designated the official state grass of Colorado in 1987, blue gamma grass can be found in meadows such as those in Moraine Park.

BLUE JOINT

Calamagrostis canadensis
Grass family (Poaceae)
Quick ID: full drooping heads

In late summer, the full heads of blue joint bow gracefully, filling the meadows of Kawuneeche Valley.

NEEDLE AND THREAD

Hesperostipa comata
Grass family (Poaceae)
Quick ID: whorls of long threads

The long thread-like projections of this grass led to the common name needle and thread. Look in meadows such as those in Moraine Park for this native perennial bunchgrass.

Enjoyed by hikers, numerous ferns line many of the trails in the park. Few people realize that when dinosaurs walked along similar paths, they also saw many of these same fern species. Ferns and their relatives were common long before flowering plants. Ferns first appear in the fossil record over 350 million years ago, about 200 million years before the first flowering plants existed. Ferns are a group of plants that lack flowers and seeds reproducing through spores, which are usually found on the underside of their leaves, or fronds. Fern relatives also called fern allies are related to ferns as they reproduce by spores but have reduced leaves or none at all. These plants were abundant in swamplands 300 million years ago.

WESTERN BRACKEN

Pteridium aquilinum var. *pubescens*
Bracken fern family (Dennstaedtiaceae)
Quick ID: triangular fronds, 12–40," divided into round-toothed leaflets
Height: 1.5–6'

A very common fern in the park, the solitary stems of western bracken fern form dense colonies along trails and forested areas in the park. In spring, the young fronds were sometimes cooked and eaten by American Indians but studies have shown that bracken fern contains carcinogens that may cause stomach cancer.

COMMON BRITTLE FERN

Cystopteris fragilis

Wood fern family (Dryopteridaceae)

Quick ID: delicate, lance-shaped fronds, tapered at terminal end

Height: 6–12"

Common brittle fern is the most common fern in the park. Some populations grow along moist streams where people might fish for trout. Other populations grow on rocky areas and show subtle genetic differences. Found in moist, rocky sites, common brittle fern is also called fragile fern. Look for this fern along Old Fall River Road.

COMMON LADY FERN

Athyrium filix-femina
Wood fern family
(Dryopteridaceae)
Quick ID: tall lacy fronds
Height: 1–3'

A large fern, common lady fern can reach 3 feet in height. Look for the tall, lacy fronds along moist areas such as Bear Lake. The roots of lady fern were routinely used to expel worms from sufferers, but too much could cause even greater medical problems such as coma or blindness.

FIELD HORSETAIL

Equisetum arvense
Horsetail family (Equisetaceae)
Quick ID: scalelike, leaves that occur at whorls along stem
Height: 2–12"

Field horsetail is a member of a small group of unusual plants known as fern allies or fern relatives. The hollow stems of horsetails contain silica crystals which made them ideal for scrubbing dishes and polishing items. This property earned this plant the common name scouring rush. Found throughout the park in wet areas look for horsetails in Endovalley Picnic Area.

AMERICAN ROCKBRAKE

Cryptogramma acrostichoides
Maidenhair fern family (Pteridaceae)
Quick ID: fan-shaped, branching, fronds with separate fertile fingerlike projections
Height: 1–7.5"

It is easy to imagine how this fern received the name rockbrake, as it commonly grows in cracks in rocks, giving the appearance that this gentle plant caused the rock to crack and break. You can see this fern on rocks along the Lily Lake Trail.

ROCKY MOUNTAIN SPIKEMOSS

Selaginella scopulorum
Spike moss family (Selaginellaceae)
Quick ID: linear; dense linear spiral-like leaves
Height: 0.4–1"

Forming mats on dry rocky areas of the park, Rocky Mountain spikemoss is not really a moss but rather a primitive fern relative. Look for this spikemoss near Lumpy Ridge.

Mosses are known as nonvascular plants, as they do not contain a defined system of vessels to carry water and nutrients. Without an internal support system, they cannot grow more than a few inches tall. They require high amounts of moisture and are found in damp areas. Mosses have been used for wound dressings and even as diapers by American Indians.

COPPER WIRE MOSS

Pohlia nutans

Pohlia moss family (Bryaceae)

Quick ID: drooping spore capsules, twisted coppery stems

A widespread species, copper wire moss occurs from dry to moist habitats. The twisting stems are a great clue to help identify it. Look for this moss along moist trails in the park such as East Inlet Trail.

HAIRY SCREW MOSS

Syntrichia ruralis

Harsh environment moss family (Pottiaceae)

Quick ID: thin, translucent, recurved leaves with long hairlike tip

Often overlooked, the various forms and shapes of mosses are fascinating. Like most mosses, hairy screw mosses are less than an inch tall but up close, they look like a forest of tiny Lilliputian trees. You can see this moss in Wild Basin.

A lichen is actually two organisms that grow together as one living entity. In a mutually beneficial relationship, a fungus provides shelter and an algae photosynthesizes the sun's energy. Sharing resources, the two can live in areas where neither could grow alone. Lichens absorb dust and other particulate matter from the air, and this is how they obtain nutrients. This also makes them very sensitive and exposed to whatever is carried in the air. Lichens are well-known indicators of air pollution.

Lichens appear in many forms and colors growing on rocks, trees, and soil. Leafy lichens are called foliose. Others have bushy structures and are called fruticose. Some that are flattened and attached to the substrate in the middle are called umbilicate. The flat crustose lichens grow on rocks so tightly they cannot be easily peeled off. Many do not have established common names, and recent efforts to familiarize them have lead to imaginative names such as pixie cups or sunburst lichens.

Lichens may represent many of the earth's oldest life forms, with some recorded at well over 4,500 years old. Lichens grow very slowly, and some, like the map lichens, are used to determine the age of geologic events such as glacial retreat. Some lichens are used as a food source. The rock tripes are often considered survival food. They have also been used to make colorful dyes for many materials, including baskets and clothing. Lichens are used traditionally to dye wool for the distinctive Harris tweeds. Some lichens such as *Usnea* have antibacterial properties, and many species are being studied for their medicinal properties. Animals such as deer, elk, and moose eat lichens, and hummingbirds and other birds use them for nesting material. Lichens eventually crumble the rocks they grow on and so are considered an important stage in the process of soil making.

PEBBLED PIXIE CUP

Cladonia pyxidata

Pixie cup lichen family (Cladoniaceae)

Quick ID: ½" trumpets with green crust

These vase-shaped fruticose lichens are often found on open ground or on decaying wood. Look in forested areas of the park for this lichen.

TUNDRA WHITEWORM LICHEN

Thamnolia subuliformis

Moisture loving lichen family (Icmadophilaceae)

Quick ID: white-worm or coral-like shape

This lichen is often seen on the tundra and can look like tiny bleached bones. Look for this lichen at Medicine Bow Curve and Rock Cut.

ORANGE ROCK POSY

Rhizoplaca chrysoleuca

Rock posy lichen family (Lecanoraceae)

Quick ID: resembling clusters of small, orange pumpkin pies

Each little pumpkin in the posy of pumpkin pies is the fruiting body of the mushroom associate of the lichen. Many lichens such as the orange rock posy can be seen growing on rocks along Trail Ridge Road.

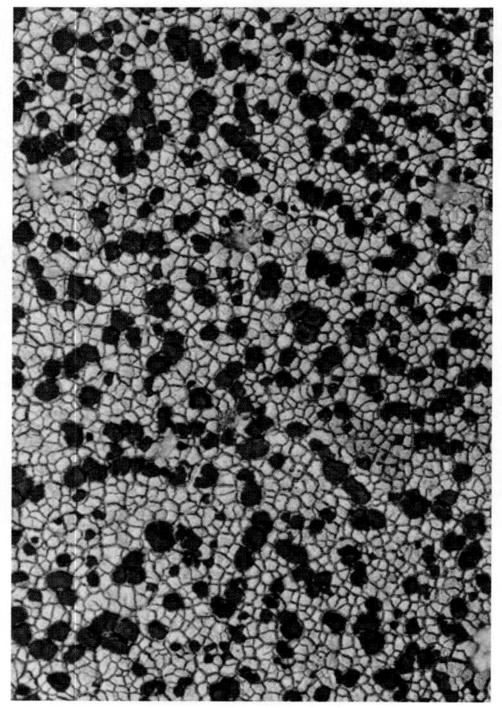

TILE LICHEN

Lecidea tessellata

Disk and tile lichen family (Lecideaceae)

Quick ID: flat black and gray tiles

These crustose lichens adhere tightly to the rocks on which they grow, resembling granite tiles on a walkway. Lily Lake Trail is a good place to see tile lichens growing on the rocks.

POWDERED BEARD LICHEN

Usnea lapponica

Shield lichen family (Parmeliaceae)

Quick ID: light green-gray, stringy, branched, hanging from trees

Some lichens such as *Usnea* have antibacterial properties, and many species are being studied for their medicinal properties. Kawuneeche Valley areas are good places to see powdered beard lichens.

SPECKLED HORSEHAIR LICHEN

Bryoria fuscenscens

Shield lichen family (Parmeliaceae)

Quick ID: dark, stringy strands hanging from trees

So similar to strands of long dark hair, this lichen is often mistaken for hair from a large mammal that has been caught on a branch. Try to spot this lichen along Onahu Creek Trail.

COMMON FRECKLE PELT

Peltigera aphthosa

Pelt lichen family (Peltigeraceae)

Quick ID: green leaf-like, black freckles, on ground

Also called dog lichen, the common freckle pelt lichen was once used to treat rabies. Look for the common freckle pelt lichen growing on the ground along the Tonahutu Spur Trail.

YELLOW MAP LICHEN

Rhizocarpon geographicum

Map lichen family (Rhizocarpaceae)

Quick ID: yellow tiles, black central dot

Pieced together like a stone walkway, the yellow map lichen grows very slowly. Map lichens are used to determine the age of geologic events such as glacial retreat. Yellow map lichens can be seen along Trail Ridge Road near the Beaver Ponds area.

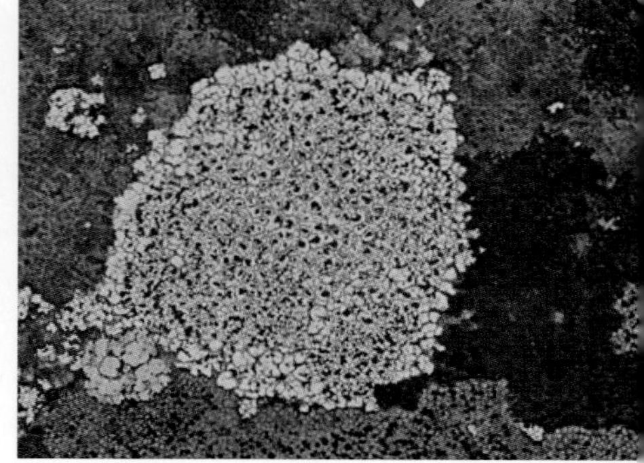

ELEGANT SUNBURST LICHEN

Xanthoria sorediata

Sunburst lichen family (Teloschistaceae)

Quick ID: bright orange patches on rock

Colorful sunburst lichens often grow around the vicinity of pika colonies and bird roosts, as they grow best in nutrient rich environments that are well fertilized. These lichens can be easily seen at Rock Cut along Trail Ridge Road.

BLISTERED ROCK TRIPE

Umbilicaria hyperborea

Umbilicate family (Umbilicariaceae)

Quick ID: dark lavalike surface with drops of small wrinkled gummy drops

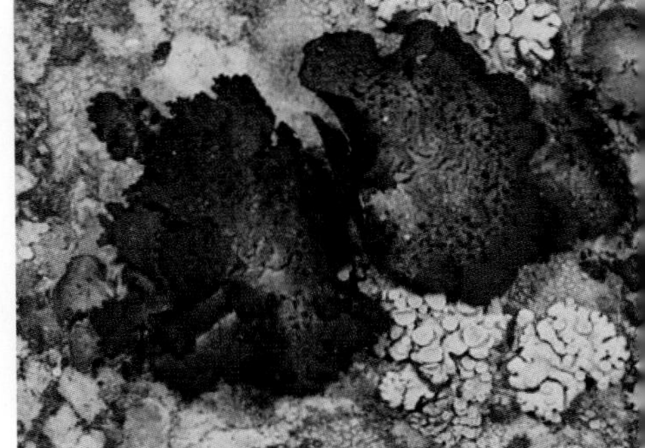

The rock tripes are often considered survival food, but those who have tried them have likened the taste and texture to tough cardboard. See these lichens attached to rocks in many areas of the park including along Trail Ridge Road.

Neither plant nor animal, mushrooms are classified in the Kingdom Fungi along with molds, mildews, and the fungal infection between your toes called athlete's foot. With names such as toadstools, dead man's fingers, and death angel it is no wonder that some people think of mushrooms as vile, slimy, poisonous objects to be avoided. Fungi however play a vital role in the ecosystem as important decomposers breaking down the dead matter of other organisms. Many plants depend on fungi in a mutually beneficial association called a mycorrhizal relationship.

Many wild animals depend on mushrooms as a source of food, therefore it is illegal for humans to pick any mushroom in Rocky Mountain National Park.

FRIENDLY AGARIC

Agaricus amicosus

Agaricus family (Agaricaceae)

Quick ID: whitish, scurfy rusty cap, skirt like white ring

Found at high elevations under conifers, this medium-large mushroom is fairly common in the park. It apparently has a rather small species range and is possibly restricted to the southern Rocky Mountains. One of the main identifying characteristics of this mushroom is that it bruises red where you touch it and has a fruity smell. The friendly agaric is in the same family as many of the "button" mushrooms that are sold in supermarkets. The fruiting body appears in August and September under spruce and subalpine fir. *Amicus* is Latin for "friend" and *osus* means "abundance."

FLY AGARIC

Amanita muscaria

Amanita family (Amanitaceae)

Quick ID: large, red cap with white spots, white stalk

Known throughout the world as the mystical fungus of fairy tales, *Amanita muscaria* is the most widely recognized member of the fungal world. The name *Amanita muscaria* is thought to come from the fact that it was used as an insecticide, as the Latin word *musca* means "fly." In some cultures, the mushroom has religious significance and has been identified in mythological tales due to its biologically active agents. Toxic doses may be as little as one cap. Please remember that collection of mushrooms in Rocky Mountain National Park is illegal.

KING BOLETE

Boletus edulis

Bolete family (Boletaceae)

Quick ID: cap 2½–8" yellowish to reddish brown, thick stalk

For fungiphiles (mushroom lovers), mushroom hunting is like a treasure hunt, and for many the king bolete is the grand prize of the fungi world. A favorite edible mushroom, it is often sautéed in butter or dried and used in soups, gravies, or as a flavoring. As with all mushrooms, proper identification is absolutely vital, and the same mushroom that may be a culinary delight to one person can make the next person violently ill (or worse). King boletes are capable of growing in soils that have been contaminated with heavy metals, which can accumulate in the mushroom. In the park, please leave the mushrooms for the wildlife that need the fruits of the fungal world to survive the harsh winters.

WESTERN PAINTED BOLETE

Suillius lakei

Bolete family (Boletaceae)

Quick ID: reddish brown with scruff on cap

Members of the genus *Suillius* are often nicknamed "Slippery Jack," as their cap is often slimy. The cap of western painted bolete is fairly sticky but not extremely slimy. Instead of gills, boletes have pores under the cap where the spores reside. Western painted bolete is only found growing near Douglas-fir. As with many fungi, it has a mutualistic relationship with Douglas-firs called a mycorrhizal relationship. The fungus supplies the tree with nutrients that it could not get on its own. In return, the tree supplies the fungus with food in the form of sugars.

ORANGE CORAL FUNGUS

Ramaria largentii

Coral and club fungi family (Clavariaceae)

Quick ID: orange, fleshy, coral-like form

Even though it looks like it would be more at home in the ocean, the orange coral fungus grows in rich, moist woods. Coral fungi look like coral, but they are soft and fleshy. Coral fungi come in a wide variety of colors from purple to red to bright orange. When ingested, the orange coral fungus is said to have a very unpleasant laxative effect on some people. Look for this and other fungi along Glacier Gorge Trail.

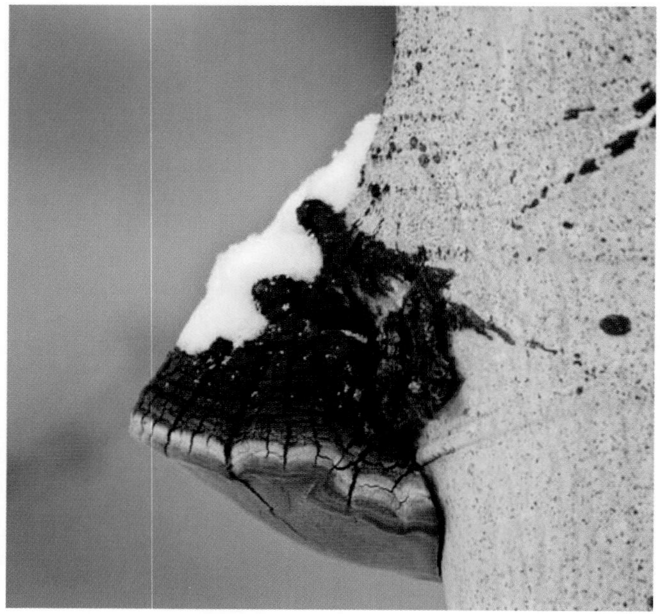

ASPEN CONK

Phellinus tremulae

White rot family (Hymenochaetaceae)

Quick ID: hoof-shaped, black and rough on top, only found on aspens

Conks are also known as bracket or shelf fungi since they are found growing on the bark of trees as shelf-like adornments. The fungus eventually kills aspens from the inside out in a disease known as heart rot. Decaying trees are often invaded by insects, which are then eaten by birds such as woodpeckers. Woodpeckers may also chisel a nest cavity in which to raise their young. Afterward, other animals such as squirrels and chipmunks may use the abandoned nest cavity. American Indians mixed the ashes of these and similar conks with tobacco products to enhance their stimulant effect.

DEADLY GALERINA

Galerina autumnalis

Galerina family (Hymenogastraceae)

Quick ID: brown, fleshy ring (annulus) on stem, found on decaying wood

Although many wild mushrooms are choice edibles, this particular mushroom is one that needs to be avoided at all costs. Widespread and quite common, deadly galerina is a small brown nondescript mushroom that grows on well-decayed wood. Usually no more than 2 inches tall, it often is passed over by mushroom foragers as being too small to supply a meal, a lucky circumstance considering it is deadly poisonous. Unfortunately, deadly galerina can be mistakenly identified by those seeking hallucinogenic mushrooms. Even one tiny bite is enough to kill a person. Several sayings about mushroom hunting have been erroneously passed down through generations, including the false tradition that any mushroom that grows on wood is edible. That could be a fatal fable.

MONTANE PUFFBALL

Calbovista subsculpta

Lycoperdon family (Lycoperdaceae)

Quick ID: white to brown, softball-size, warty surface, sterile base

Puffballs are generally round, marble- to basketball-size masses of spores. Many puffballs are edible, including the montane puffball. The outer covering is tough and covered with feltlike warts, but when young, the puffball's inside is white with a rather firm consistency similar to angel food cake. Many puffballs are called gasteromycetes, which comes from the Latin word *gaster,* meaning "stomach," and recipes for young puffballs abound. As puffballs mature they lose their palatability as the spore mass turns yellowish, then brown and powdery. Mature puffballs eventually open, and the spores are whisked away by the wind. Please remember that it is illegal to pick mushrooms in Rocky Mountain National Park.

ROCKY MOUNTAIN RUSSULA

Russula montana

Russula family (Russulaceae)

Quick ID: red cap, white gills, thick white stalk

Russulas are a family of mushrooms that add color to the forest floor as they often sport brightly colored caps. The brittle gills flake off like almond flakes. About 200 species of russulas have been documented in North America, and unfortunately, many of them are extremely difficult to identify correctly. Some of the caps, including those of Rocky Mountain russula, have a hot, peppery taste, which indicates that they should be avoided. Only a few russulas are edible, and many will cause extreme gastrointestinal reactions, so they are best avoided.

Galls are unusual growths on plants formed when the plant's tissue overreacts to a stimulant such as a bacteria, virus, fungus, or insect. The causative agent is very specific for the plant, and like a person having an allergic reaction, the plant overcompensates for the irritation. In the case of galls, the cells of the plant are induced to grow in unusual ways. Galls may take the form of lumps, warts, balls, finger-like projections, or clusters of leaves. They can be fuzzy, smooth, or spiny, and they display a wide range of colors. A common type of gall forms when insects lay their eggs on a plant and larvae hatch and tunnel into the plant. The plant overreacts and begins to rapidly grow thick tissue around the invader. The larvae spend the winter in the shelter of the gall. In spring, they chew their way out of the gall, pupate, and then fly away as adults. Even though the plant may form galls, these usually do not affect the health of the plant.

COOLEY SPRUCE GALL APHID

Aldelges cooleyei

Adelgid family (Adelgidae)

Quick ID: brown, spruce cone appearance on spruce and Douglas-fir

Size: 1-3"

The Cooley spruce gall aphid is a native pest that primarily infests blue, Engelmann and Sitka spruce and Douglas-fir. Galls caused by this insect are elongated, 1 to 3 inches long, and resemble a spruce cone. The actual life cycle is complicated, with different morphs appearing over a two-year span, including one female-only generation, which produces virgin-birth young in a process called parthenogenesis.

MAPLE ERINEUM MITE

Eriophyes calaceris

Eriophyes family (Eriophyidae)

Quick ID: pinkish-red blotches on maple leaves

Size: varies with leaf

As Rocky Mountain maple leaves are developing, a small mite called the maple erineum mite begins its life cycle. Its feeding activity stimulates velvety reddish hairs to form an intriguing leaf gall within the tissues of the maple leaf. The mites live and reproduce in the galls during the summer, then move out to overwinter under bark scales before the leaves are shed in the autumn.

ROSY CHEEKED WILLOW APPLE GALL

Pontania pomum

Sawfly family (Tenthredinidae)

Quick ID: yellowish to rosy red fleshy round growths on willows

Size: ⅓"

Rosy cheeked willow apple gall is formed when a sawfly lays its egg in the willow tissue and stimulates the willow to form yellowish-red round galls that resemble tiny apples. The plant responds to the irritating stimulus from the insect by cell enlargement, which causes the abnormal growths. The sawfly larva develops inside the spherical fleshy gall.

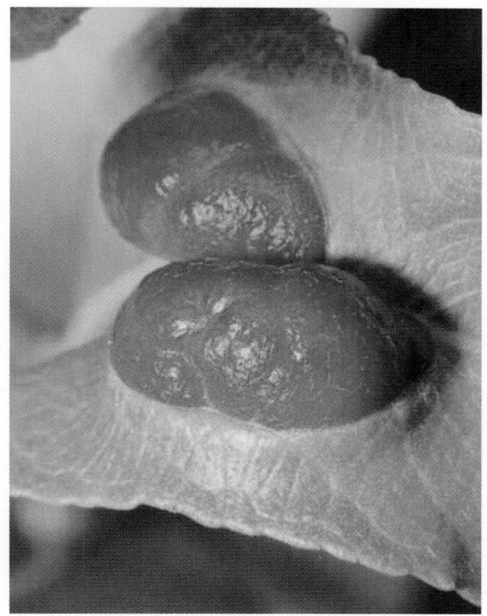

ROSY RED WILLOW GALL

Pontania sp.
Sawfly family (Tenthredinidae)
Quick ID: warty red blisters on willow leaves
Size: ½-1"

Rosy red willow gall is formed when a sawfly, *Pontania* sp., deposits an egg in willow tissue causing a benign cancerous-like growth to form and become engulfed by the leaf. These galls are often seen on high-altitude willows in the alpine area of the park.

WILLOW CONE GALL MIDGE

Rabdophaga strobiloides
Gall midge family (Cecidomyiidae)
Quick ID: greenish yellow to brown, pineconelike growth on willows
Size: 1–1.5"

This common gall looks very much like a pinecone growing on a willow. The unusual galls harbor the larva of a small fly called a midge. In spring, the adults deposit an egg into the developing terminal bud. After the egg hatches, the bud leaves develop into a mass of flattened scales that resemble a pinecone. Common gall larvae remain in the willows until the following spring, when they hatch out as adults.

Glossary

Alkaloid: bitter compounds produced by plants to discourage predators

Alluvial fan: fan-shaped unconsolidated materials deposited from an inland flood

Alpine: treeless ecosystem above 11,000 to 11,500 feet

Alternate leaves: growing singly on a stem without an opposite leaf

Anther: tip of a flower's stamen that produces pollen grains

Basal: at the base

Boreal forest: subarctic coniferous forest just below the tundra

Bulb: underground structure made up of layered, fleshy scales

Cache: storage area of food

Capsule: a dry fruit that releases seeds through splits or holes

Carrion: remains of deceased animal

Catkin: a spike, either upright or drooping, of tiny flowers

Cirque: semicircular head of a glaciated valley

Compound leaf: a leaf that is divided into two or more leaflets

Corm: rounded, solid underground stem

Cryptic: coloration that allows concealment or camouflage

Deciduous: a tree that seasonally loses its leaves

Diurnal: active by day

Drupe: fleshy fruit usually having a single hard pit that encloses a seed

Ecosystem: a biological environment consisting of all the living organisms in a particular area as well as the nonliving components such as water, soil, air, and sunlight

Ethnobotany: the study of the relationship between plants and people

Evergreen: a tree that keeps its leaves (often needles) year-round

Genus: taxonomic rank below family and above species; always capitalized and italicized

Glacier: a persistent body of ice

Glean: pick small insects from foliage

Habitat: the area or environment where an organism lives or occurs

Hawking: hunting while flying

Hover-glean: to forage while fluttering in the air

Introduced: a species living outside its native range; often introduced by human activity

Krummholz: dwarfed conifers that form shrubby growth patterns due to inhospitable conditions near the alpine timberline; from German for "crooked wood"

Leaflet: a part of a compound leaf; may resemble an entire leaf, but it is borne on a vein of a leaf rather than the stem. Leaflets are referred to as pinnae; compound leaves are pinnate (featherlike)

Local resident: nonmigratory species found year-round in an area; also "resident"

Metamorphic rock: a rock such as gneiss, schist, or quartzite that has been altered by extreme heat and pressure

Migrate: movement of birds between breeding grounds and wintering areas

Montane: referring to the mountainous region; ecosystem from 5,600 to 9,500 feet

Mutualism: a type of symbiosis where both organisms benefit

Mycelium: mass of hyphae or fungus filaments

Mycorrhiza: (pl. mycorrhizae) the symbiotic association of fungal mycelium and the root ends of trees or other plants

Nape: area at back of the head

Native: a species indigenous or endemic to an area

Nectar: sweet liquid produced by flowers to attract pollinators

Niche: an organism's response to available resources and competitors (like a human's job)

Nitrogen fixation: process by which atmospheric nitrogen is converted by bacteria that reside in plant root nodules into nitrogen compounds that help the plant grow

Nocturnal: active at night

Omnivore: feeds on a variety of foods including both plant and animal materials

Opposite leaves: growing in pairs along the stem

Parasitism: one organism benefits at the expense of another organism

Pinnate: divided or lobed along each side of a leaf stalk, resembling a feather

Pollen: small, powdery particles that contain the plant's male sex cells

Pollination: transfer of pollen from an anther (male) to a stigma (female)

Primaries: outermost flight feathers of a bird's wing

Riparian: area located on the bank of a river or stream

Rhizome: underground stem that grows horizontally and sends up shoots

Sepal: usually green leaf-like structures found underneath the flower

Species: taxonomic rank below genus; always italicized but never capitalized; also called "specific epithet"

Stamen: male part of a flower composed of a filament, or stalk, and anther, the sac at the tip of the filament that produces pollen

Subalpine: ecosystem from 9,000 to 11,000 feet; regions below timberline

Symbiosis: association of unlike organisms that benefits one or both

Taxonomy: study of scientific classifications

Toothed: jagged or serrated edge

Torpor: short-term state of decreased physiological activity including reduced body temperature and metabolic rate

Tree line: the area between forest and tundra; timberline; often with krummholz

Tundra: a biome where harsh conditions prohibit tree growth

Wing bar: line of contrastingly colored plumage formed by the tips of the flight feathers of birds

Winged: thin, flattened expansion on the sides of a plant part

Useful References

Angel, L. 2005. *Butterflies of Rocky Mountain National Park: An Observer's Guide.* Boulder, CO: Johnson Books; Big Earth Publishing.

Armstrong, D. M. 2008. *Rocky Mountain Mammals: A Handbook of Mammals of Rocky Mountain National Park and Vicinity.* 3rd ed. In cooperation with The Rocky Mountain Nature Association, Estes Park, CO.; Boulder, CO: University Press of Colorado.

Beidleman, L. H., R. G. Beidleman, B. E. Willard. 2000. *Plants of Rocky Mountain National Park.* Helena, MT: Rocky Mountain Nature Association and Falcon Publishing.

Benedict, A. D. 2008. *The Naturalist's Guide to the Southern Rockies.* Golden, CO: Fulcrum Publishing.

Brinkley, E. S. 2008. *Field Guide to Birds of North America.* New York, NY: Sterling Publishing Co.

Carter, J. L. 2006. *Trees and Shrubs of Colorado.* Silver City, NM: Mimbres Publishing.

Cranshaw, W., B. Kondratieff. 2006. *Guide to Colorado Insects.* Englewood, CO: Westcliffe Publishers.

Dannen, K.and D. Dannen. 2002. *Best East Day Hikes Rocky Mountain National Park.* 1st ed. Guilford, CT: Globe Pequot Press /FalconGuides.

——— 2002. *Hiking Rocky Mountain National Park.* 9th ed. Guilford, CT: Globe Pequot Press/ FalconGuides.

Ells, J. 2006. *Rocky Mountain Flora.* Golden, CO: Colorado Mountain Club Press.

Emerick, J. C. 1995. *Rocky Mountain National Park Natural History Handbook.* Estes Park, CO: Rocky Mountain Nature Association.

Evenson, V. S. 1997. *Mushrooms of Colorado and the Southern Rocky Mountains.* Denver, CO: Denver Botanic Gardens.

Forsyth, A. 2006. *Mammals of North America: Temperate and Arctic Regions.* Buffalo, NY: Firefly Books.

Gunn, J., ed. 2001. *Field Guide to Wildlife Viewing in Rocky Mountain National Park.* Estes Park, CO: Rocky Mountain Nature Association.

Hailman, J. P. and E. D. Hailman. 2003. *Hiking Circuits in Rocky Mountain National Park.* Boulder, CO: University Press of Colorado.

Malitz, J. 2008. *Rocky Mountain National Park Dayhiker's Guide.* Boulder, CO: Johnson Books, Big Earth Publishing Company.

Mathews, D. 2003. *Rocky Mountain Natural History Grand Teton to Jasper.* Portland, OR: Raven Editions.

Robertson, L. 1999. *Southern Rocky Mountain Wildflowers.* Helena, MT: Falcon Publishing.

Roederer, S. 2002. *Birding Rocky Mountain National Park.* Boulder, CO: Johnson Publishing.

Sibley, D. A. 2000. *National Audubon Society The Sibley Guide to Birds.* 1st ed. New York: Chanticleer Press.

Weber, W. A. 1976. *Rocky Mountain Flora.* 5th ed. Niwot, CO: University Press of Colorado.

Wilkinson, T. 1994. *Rocky Mountain National Park A Wildlife Watcher's Guide.* Minocqua, WI: North Word Press.

Wilson, D. E. and S. Ruff, eds. 1999. *The Smithsonian Book of North American Mammals.* Washington, D.C.: Smithsonian Institution

Zwinger, A. H. and B. E. Willard. 1996. *Land Above the Trees: A Guide to American Alpine Tundra.* Boulder, CO: Johnson Publishing.

Index

About the Authors

As professional photographers, biologists, and authors, Ann and Rob Simpson are noted national park experts, having spent years involved with research and interpretation in the national parks. They have written numerous books on national parks coast to coast that promote wise and proper use of natural habitats and environmental stewardship. As a former chief of interpretation and a national park board member, Rob has a unique understanding of the inner workings of the national park system. In cooperation with American Park Network, the Simpsons have led Canon "Photography in the Parks" workshops in major national parks, including Grand Canyon, Yellowstone, Yosemite, and Great Smokies.

Ann and Rob are both award-winning biology professors at Lord Fairfax Community College in Middletown, Virginia. With a background in science education, Ann heads the science department, and as part of the college's nature photography curriculum, the Simpson's regularly lead international photo tours to parks and natural-history destinations around the world. The Simpsons are both members of the Virginia Outdoor Writers Association, the Mason-Dixon Outdoor Writers Association, and the North American Nature Photography Association.

Long known for their stunning images of the natural world, their work has been widely published in magazines such as *National Geographic, Time Magazine, National Wildlife,* and *Ranger Rick* as well as in many calendars, postcards, and books. You can see their work at Simpson's Nature Photography at www.agpix.com/snphotos.